THE ULTIMATE QUEST

The Ultimate Quest

Uncovering the True Location of Paradise

ROBERT LAZU KMITA

Angelico Press

First published in the USA
by Angelico Press 2026

For information, address:
Angelico Press, Ltd.
169 Monitor St.
Brooklyn, NY 11222
www.angelicopress.com

ppr 979-8-89280-171-3
cloth 979-8-89280-172-0
ebook 979-8-89280-173-7

Book and cover design
by Michael Schrauzer

To my noble friend,
Horia-Roman Patapievici

"I trust I make myself obscure."
(Saint Thomas More)

CONTENTS

FOREWORD

In 2017, the magazine *Orizont* published, across five large pages, a text signed by one of the most brilliant Romanian intellectuals of recent decades, Horia-Roman Patapievici. When I read it on the cover of the twelfth issue from that winter, the title of Patapievici's article electrified me instantly: "Where Has Paradise Gone?" A master of words, the author knew how to formulate the question in a way that makes you stop and think. The nuance captured by the question suggested the attitude of pearl-making shell creatures which, when sensing the approach of danger, close themselves hermetically, hiding their priceless core. Like a pearl, Paradise *was not* only hidden from us—*it hid itself.* For, as Horia-Roman Patapievici brilliantly suggests, Paradise is profoundly bound in solidarity with the supreme being God who, offended by the terrible transgression of the proto-parents Adam and Eve, concealed the jewel from those contaminated by the deadly radiation of Luciferian sin.

Such topics seem today, more than ever, outdated. The intellectual leaders of the materialist-evolutionist paradigm smile ironically, often even scornfully, whenever someone mentions the ancient histories of the Sacred Books of the Holy Scripture of the Judeo-Christian tradition. Labeled as "myths," "fables," or the "products of the poetic imagination" of primitives who emerged from the lower species from which they evolved, these accounts have been almost entirely excluded from classrooms and intellectual forums shaped by fashionable influencers. Who today still troubles themselves with the historical, real existence of Paradise?

If in the "free" Western world such concerns are at best accidental, in a post-communist country like Romania, theological-metaphysical reflections of this kind are practically nonexistent. The courage of Horia-Roman Patapievici to write and publish such a text deserves emphasis. Even more so because, although situated within a broad cultural perspective—one in which great poets and writers like Dante, Eminescu, Pound, and Culianu are invited into the discussion—he does not speak *from outside* the subject, out of mere curiosity, but *from within it*, animated by his Christian faith. This was made clear by Patapievici in the small monograph that naturally followed his article in *Orizont*. His volume, titled *Two Essays on Paradise and a Conclusion* (2019), is a true testimony of his faith.

Encouraged and inspired, then, by Patapievici's bold act and by his refined speculations—in which

Dante's ascent toward the world of pure intelligences plays the key role—I dared to pull from the archives of notes gathered over more than thirty years of reading all the quotations that formed the texture of my own study.

Playing the role of an improvised Sherlock Holmes, I began by exploring the texts of those who believed that physical traces of Paradise's existence were still accessible in our world. Eager to protect and support the literal interpretation of the Bible, Saint Augustine is the church doctor at the origin of this vision. Among others, Saints Isidore of Seville and Thomas Aquinas shared it. Through various intermediary sources, Admiral Christopher Columbus inherited it as well. The discoverer of the New World was convinced that he had passed near the region where, protected by inaccessible heights, lay the land of youth-without-old-age and life-without-death. He left substantial traces of this conviction in his letters. Although it differed from the vision of the Angelic Doctor—who believed Paradise was surrounded by a protective wall of fire—Admiral Columbus thought Paradise existed in our world, atop a mountain forbidden to mortals.

The fundamental error of such a vision, today, can no longer be concealed. The meticulous explorations of recent centuries, conducted with increasingly sophisticated means, show clearly that no such forbidden place exists anywhere in the physical world accessible to us. From this realization to skepticism, and then to unbelief, the road has unfortunately not been long. Thus it happens that today we see cardinals and bishops of the Catholic Church publicly claiming that Paradise is nothing more than a "myth" with moral purposes. For them — as for most people today — the word "myth" is synonymous with "lie." A beautiful one, poetic even, and perhaps with valuable moral content, but still a lie. Well, I will not hide that, for my part, I consider Paradise more real — and certainly true — than our own world. Yet explaining this is not easy.

After completing the journey through the texts of those saints and church doctors convinced that the literal reading of Genesis is the one to follow, I began my sortie into the world of ideas of those who believed, on the contrary, that only the allegorical, mystical, symbolic interpretation of the texts revealed the true history of Paradise. Saints such as Ambrose of Milan, Gregory of Nyssa, Athanasius the Great, Gregory of Nazianzus, and Maximus the Confessor guided me toward an understanding that reached full maturity only in the past year. Article by article, it gradually became clearer.

I discovered several metaphor-symbols through which I tried to describe the essence of the understanding I attained: Paradise lies in a history before history. It was accessible—ontologically speaking—in a condition of nature, both human and cosmological, that represented its defining note. This condition was available through the sanctifying grace with which God enveloped the world and humankind at the beginning. The "Fall" meant the loss of both this grace and the qualities of that world. In this volume you will be able to read the first version of the explanation I propose in answer to Horia-Roman Patapievici's question, "Where Has Paradise Gone?," discovering details that, I hope, are delightful and surprising. I announce from the start that, with God's help, one more volume will follow—just as short but, I believe, definitive. I hope to thus complete the depiction of that most complete picture of the origins and meanings of universal history.

This first volume, whose publication I owe to Mr John Riess and Angelico Press, is based on a significant number of articles published in three periodicals. The first is the American Catholic newspaper *The Remnant*, where in 2019 I published six essays. I owe its enthusiastic editor, Michael J. Matt, my warmest thanks. Shortly after *The*

Remnant began publishing the articles, the critic and writer Mircea Mihăieș invited me to publish a series of eight articles, "Return to Paradise," in *Orizont* cultural magazine. My gratitude for such encouraging support is boundless. Finally, I also thank Dr Joseph Shaw, who published an essay on the same topic in the distinguished journal *Gregorius Magnus* of the Una Voce Federation. And to Horia-Roman Patapievici, the one who inspired this project from the very beginning, I send all my gratitude along with this first paradisiacal volume, accompanied by a special dedication.

Robert Lazu Kmita

CHAPTER 1

The Incredible Discovery of Christopher Columbus

Recorded by the Dominican Father Bartolomé de las Casas in the *History of the Indies* (1561), Christopher Columbus's testimony is marked by an easily noticeable emotional crescendo. The excitement that permeates the admiral's words is driven by his conviction that the nights preceding August 16, 1498, foretold the approach of a crucial moment of his third expedition to the New World:

> And he says each night he was marveling at such a change in the heavens, and of the temperature there, so near the equinoctial line, which he experienced in all this voyage, after having found land; especially the sun being in Leo, where, as has been told, in the mornings a loose gown was worn, and where the people of that place—Gracia—were

> actually whiter than the people who have been seen in the Indies.[1]

Everything on that day, August 16, heralded that something extraordinary was going to happen. After sailing—"praised be the Lord"—more than twenty-six leagues on a sea as calm as the mirror of a celestial lake, Columbus observed

> a wonderful thing, that when he left the Canaries for this Española, having gone 300 leagues to the west, then the needles declined to the northeast one quarter, and the North Star did not rise but 5 degrees, and now in this voyage it has not declined to the northwest until last night, when it declined more than a quarter and a half, and some needles declined a half which are two quarters; and this happened suddenly last night.[2]

---

[1] Julius E. Olson and Edward G. Bourne, eds., *The Northmen*, Columbus and Cabot, 985–1503 (New York: Charles Scribner's Sons, 1906), 363. Written between 1527 and 1561, the text of *Historia de las Indias* itself has such an amazing history that numerous pages would be needed to depict it entirely. I will quote here the Spanish original text: "Y dice que cadano che estaban sobre el aviso maravillándose de tanto mudamiento del cielo, y de la temperancia dél, allí, tan cerca de la línea equinoccial, en todo este viaje, despues de haber hallado la tierra; mayormente estando el sol en Leo, donde, como arriba ha dicho, por las mañanas se vestia un ropon, y la gente de allí de Gracia ser más blancos que otros que haya visto en las Indias." Bartolomé de las Casas, *Historia de las Indias*, vol. 2 (Madrid: Migel Ginesta, 1875), 314.

[2] Olson and Bourne, *The Northmen*, 363. "Dice aquí una cosa maravillosa, que cuando partía de Canaria para esta Española,

Yet, it was not until the following day, Friday, August 17, 1498, after he had traversed more than thirty-seven leagues on a calm sea, that the admiral realized the epochal event that had just occurred:

> He says that not finding islands now, assures him that that land from whence he came is a vast mainland, *or where the Earthly Paradise is*, "because all say that it is at the end of the east, and this is the Earthly Paradise," says he.[3]

Narrated in terms of disconcerting simplicity, the presumed crossing of a region where the earthly Paradise hypothetically was thought to be located did not arouse any suspicion or skeptical questions in the mind of the narrator, Father Bartolomé de las Casas, just as it did not stir even the slightest shadow of doubt in the navigator's mind. In fact, for both of them and for most of their contemporaries, the historical, real, and tangible existence of Paradise was an unquestionable fact. The only

pasando 300 leguas al Oueste, luego nordesteaban las agujas una cuarta, y la estrella del Norte no se alzaba sino 5°, y ahora en este viaje nunca le ha nordesteado, hasta anoche, que nordesteaba más de una cuarta y media, y algunas agujas nordesteaban medio viento, que son dos cuartas; y esto fué, todo de golpe, anoche." De las Casas, *Historia de las Indias*, 314.

[3] Olson and Bourne, *The Northmen*, 364–65. "Dice, que con no hallar ya islas se certifica, que aquella tierra de donde viene sea gran tierra firme, oá donde está el Paraíso terrenal." De las Casas, *Historia de las Indias*, 315.

unresolved issue remained the geographical position of the garden where "youth without old age and life without death" could be found.

Christopher Columbus did not spare any effort to decipher the enigma of the historical Paradise, recorded in the book of Genesis. As a proof of his keen interest in finding the terrestrial Paradise, we can read the numerous pages dedicated to this subject in his letter dated (around) May 30, 1498, sent to Their Royal Highnesses King Ferdinand II of Aragon and Queen Isabella I of Castile.

One might say that all the intellectual authorities of the era are invited to this feast of theories regarding the location of the Garden of Eden. Aristotle, Strabo, Pliny, Ptolemy, Saints Ambrose, Augustine, Bede the Venerable, Isidore of Seville, and many others all attest to this firm conviction that Columbus had discovered the geographical position of Paradise—"whither no one can go but by God's permission."[4]

We could continue across many more pages the presentation of the ideas and theories of this unparalleled adventurer. However, what we have shown so far is sufficient to prove that the existence of a

[4] R. H. Major, trans., *Select Letters of Cristopher Columbus, with Original Documents, relating to his Four Voyages to the New World* (London: n.p., 1847), 137.

geographical location of Paradise where God placed Adam and Eve at the beginning of the world's history was considered, in the fifteenth century of the Christian era, *an undeniable historical fact.*

Confronted with this certainty, we can wonder what answer should be given to someone who straightforwardly asks us where Paradise is located. In one of his sermons, Saint John Chrysostom did not hesitate to pose this very question to his fellow Christians.[5] I can assure you, with full confidence, that *this* is one of those very few questions that truly deserve an answer. To discover it, we need the genius of the most brilliant minds serving the Christian Tradition.

[5] *The Homilies of Saint John Chrysostom on the Gospel of Matthew*, With Notes and Indices, Part I, Hom. I–XXV (Oxford: John Henry Parker, 1843), 14.

CHAPTER 2

The Hermeneutic Rule of Saint Augustine

In *De Civitate Dei*, Saint Augustine's final and most comprehensive theological synthesis, he discusses all the major theological themes pertinent to the Christian faith. Among the topics he addresses, the historical existence of Paradise is naturally included, which he tackles in chapter 21 of the thirteenth book of this true "summa" of Christian theology and biblical exegesis.

First, as many historians and theologians emphasize, his analysis represents the polemical stance of the great Latin doctor against the heresies of a "spiritualist" Gnostic sect, the Seleucians (already combated in his treatise *De Haeresibus*). Among other things, the members of this heterodox group denied the visible, historical existence of the Garden of Eden.[1] But despite this particular aspect, the

[1] Saint Augustine systematically criticized the teachings of Seleucians in a treatise entitled *De Haeresibus ad Quodvultdeum.*

scope of chapter 21 is much broader and deeper than merely arguing against one of the countless heresies spread at that time.

What the African bishop firmly establishes is *the non-exclusive relationship between any spiritual, allegorical interpretation of the biblical text about Paradise and its historical reference*. In other words, Saint Augustine insists that, despite the possibility of any legitimate spiritual interpretation of the sacred text, *Paradise was historical and tangible*, just as our own country or neighborhood is for us. In short, Paradise was—and it is—real. This is what we can call Saint Augustine's hermeneutical axiom.

What he strives to establish as a fundamental hermeneutic rule is the non-exclusive relationship between the spiritual dimension of allegorical readings applied to sacred texts and their historical dimension. In other words, Saint Augustine supports, on one hand, the legitimacy of spiritual-allegorical interpretations of Holy Scripture, while simultaneously emphasizing the complete truth of the historical facts narrated in the biblical texts.

He says about the Seleucians (named so from the name of their master, Seleucius), that they deny the existence of visible Paradise: "Negant etiam visibilem paradisum." Augustine, *De Haeresibus ad Quodvultdeum*, in *Patrologica Latina*, ed. Jean-Paul Migne, vol. 42, column 42.

His argument is based on one of the most important allegorical interpretations from the texts of Saint Paul: chapter 4 of the *Epistle to the Galatians*. Here, after recalling the story related in chapter 16 of the Book of Genesis—where we learn about the birth of Abraham's two sons, Ishmael and Isaac—the Apostle to the Gentiles allegorically interprets the historical persons involved. The two mothers, Hagar and Sarah, are the two covenants (verse 24), whilst the son of the slave woman, Ishmael, symbolizes those "enslaved" under the law (verse 30) and Isaac symbolizes all the children of the promise of rebirth in the "Jerusalem above" (verse 28). This essential lesson of allegorical exegesis, provided within the very pages of the Holy Book, gives Saint Augustine the foundation for his attack oriented against all those interpretations that, in the name of an exclusivist spiritual reading, eliminate the concrete, historical dimension of the sacred texts:

> But to say that there could not have been a corporeal Paradise because it can also be understood in a spiritual sense is like saying that Abraham did not have two wives, Hagar and Sarah, and two sons by them, one by the maidservant and the other by the freewoman, because the apostle says that two covenants were prefigured in them.[2]

[2] Augustine, *The City of God against the Pagans*, trans. Robert W. Dyson (Cambridge University Press, 1998), 568. "Quasi propterea

Continuing in the same vein of insistently emphasizing the historical truth of biblical events narrated in the book of Genesis, Saint Augustine adds yet another illustrious example, this time taken from chapter 17 of the book of Exodus. Here, we see Moses, threatened with stoning by an excessively thirsty people, praying to the Living God to save him from an extremely dangerous situation. Prompt and effective, Heaven's response generated the miracle of the water springing from the rock after Moses struck it with the same staff with which he had parted the Red Sea (Exodus 17, 5–6).

To deny the real, historical existence of Paradise, says Saint Augustine, "is like saying that water never flowed from the rock when Moses struck it, because the symbol of Christ can also be seen in it; for the same apostle says 'and that Rock was Christ'" (1 Corinthians 10, 4).[3]

After enumerating several allegorical interpretations—the most well known being the one saying

non potuerit esse paradisus corporalis, quia potest etiam spiritalis intellegi; tamquam ideo non fuerint duae mulieres, Agar et Sarra, et ex eis duo filii Abrahae, unus de ancilla, alius de libera, quia duo testamenta in eis figurata dicit apostolus." *Patrologia Latina*, 41, 394.

[3] Augustine, *City of God*, 568. "Aut ideo de nulla petra Moyse per cutiente aqua defluxerit, quia potest illic figurata significatione etiam Christus intellegi, eodem apostolo dicente: Petra autem erat Christus." *Patrologia Latina*, 41, 394.

that "Paradise is the Church, as we read of her in the Song of Songs [4:12ff.]; the four rivers of Paradise are the four gospels; the fruit-bearing trees are the saints, and the fruit of them is their works; the Tree of Life is the Holy of Holies, even Christ; the tree of knowledge of good and evil is our possession of free will"[4]—he will conclude by repeating the hermeneutic principle that underlies all of his interpretations:

> No one, then, forbids us *to* understand Paradise according to these, and perhaps other, more appropriate, allegorical interpretations, while also believing in the truth of that story as presented to us in a most faithful narrative of events.[5]

Simultaneously emphasizing the reality of the historical events recounted in the Bible, Saint Augustine is convinced that only in this way can both their

---

[4] Augustine, *City of God*, 568. "Possunt haec etiam in ecclesia intellegi, ut ea melius accipiam ustam quam prophetica indicia praecedentia futurorum; paradisum scilicet ipsam ecclesiam, sicut de illa legitur in cantico canticorum; quattuor autem paradisi flumina quattuor euangelia, ligna fructifera sanctos, fructus autem eorum opera eorum, lignum uitae sanctum sanctorum utique Christum, lignum scientiae boni et mali proprium voluntatis arbitrium." *Patrologia Latina*, 41, 395.

[5] Augustine, *City of God*, 568–69. "Haec et si qua alia commodius dici possunt de intellegendo spiritaliter paradiso nemine prohibente dicantur, dum tamen et illius historiae ueritas fidelissima rerum gestarum narratione commendata credatur." *Patrologia Latina*, 41, 395.

truth and their spiritual, allegorical interpretations be defended, which otherwise would be devoid of foundation and authenticity.

Guided by prudence, I believe it is necessary, as a preamble of what follows, to firmly state that what I will discuss further does not question such a requirement, which is vital for the correct understanding of the holy texts of the Old and New Testaments. However, after seeing how Saint Augustine insists on the historicity of Paradise, I also draw attention to a particular aspect, which, although not immediately apparent, inadvertently conceals one of the most subtle distortions in hermeneutical perspective. What is this?

When Augustine states that Paradise was characterized by a historical existence similar to episodes such as the birth of Ishmael by Hagar and Isaac by Sarah, or the water gushing from the rock after Moses struck it with his rod, his writing does not mention the fact that we are dealing with *two dimensions, two different stages of history*. The first, specific to that happy life lived by Adam and Eve in Eden *before* committing the original sin, is the pre-lapsarian period of history, characteristic of the world as it was before the Fall. The second dimension of history, post-lapsarian, is specific to the "fallen" world *after* the commission of the original sin. In this one we are born, and currently live. What must be made clear is that *the quality* of the original created nature—both of man and all other creatures in Paradise, as well as of the world itself—is very different from the quality of the nature of fallen man and the fallen world. As I will show in the following chapters, the difference between these two parts of history is truly significant.

If I were to propose a metaphor to illustrate, as much as possible, this ontological difference, I would invoke two substances related by structure yet radically different: graphite (carbon) and diamond. The world before the fall, like man in his original paradisiacal condition, was like a precious diamond, perfectly cut, allowing the rays of divine grace to pass through its crystalline transparency unhindered. Corrupted by the original sin and its terrible, cosmic repercussions, the world after the fall, on the other hand, became completely opaque—like graphite—to the work of the divine energies of grace.

The world created by God was beautiful and transparent, like a perfect diamond: all divine graces passed through it as through water, clear as the purest crystal. After the original sin, both human nature and the nature of all creatures, including the cosmos itself, became opaque to grace and as dark as a massive block of coal. In his Epistle to the

Romans, chapter 8, verse 20, Saint Paul describes the tragedy of the entire created nature that, unwillingly, followed man in his fall: "For the creature was made subject to vanity, not willingly, but by reason of him who subjected it." That is why, a little later, we learn from the glorious apostle that "the whole creation groaneth and travaileth in pain together until now" (Romans 8:22).

The human nature following the original sin (*status naturae lapsae*) is ontologically different from that which preceded it (*status naturae elevatae*) at this turning point in human history. To underscore the difference, it is sufficient to say that the former was immortal, while the latter state of nature—as we learn with much sorrow through the inevitable separation from loved ones—is mortal. Similarly, the world of eternal youth and life without death is completely different from the world that followed the rebellion of our first parents, Adam and Eve, against the Creator. Thus, this is the aspect insufficiently highlighted by Saint Augustine. This deficiency, due to the difficulty of addressing ethereal subjects like Paradise, will have an incalculable influence on subsequent hermeneutical traditions. Alongside Christopher Columbus, Saint Thomas Aquinas is the best-suited witness to reveal the enduring consequences of such a profound influence. Based on the proposed visual metaphor of diamond and coal, I will show in the next chapters that the difference between these two "sides" of history—*before* and *after* original sin—is indeed enormous, even though both are characterized, in different proportions and manners, by temporality and veracity. This is an aspect that any theologian or believer must consider in order to answer correctly the crucial question: where is Paradise?

In any case, neither he nor Saint Augustine would have said—like a cardinal of the Holy Roman Catholic Church did in front of TV cameras—that the account of the Garden of Eden and its first two human inhabitants, Adam and Eve, from the book of Genesis is "a beautiful, sophisticated mythological account." For the fathers and doctors of the church, as it should be for any faithful Catholic today, Paradise is real and true, while any "science" that states the opposite can only be considered deceptive or, at least, the result of ignorance. It seems that such basic truths need to be remembered by those Catholic theologians who, instead of defending the perennial truths of Holy Scripture, prefer to embrace and defend fashionable dubious theories.

CHAPTER 3

Saint Thomas Aquinas and the Geographical Location of Paradise

In a similar way to Saint Augustine, the Angelic Doctor resumes his meditation on Paradise in his final synthesis, *Summa Theologiae*—a monumental work abandoned unfinished shortly before the end of his earthly life on March 7, 1274. The principle established by Augustine as axiomatic to any interpretation related to the existence and location of earthly Paradise is vigorously reaffirmed in the context of the discussions in question 102 from the first part of this massive theological treatise. Here, from the very first article, which is entirely dedicated to the question of the corporeality of Paradise, Saint Thomas Aquinas cites in full two key passages from the works of Saint Augustine. The first passage, taken from *De Genesi ad Litteram* (*On the Literal Meaning of Genesis*), is as follows:

> I am well aware that many people have said many things about Paradise. There are, however, three generally held opinions about this topic; one held by those who think Paradise should be understood in the literal material sense, another by those for whom only the spiritual sense is true, the third by those who take Paradise in each way, differently though in the material, differently in the spiritual sense. So then, in a word, I admit that it is the third opinion which I favor.[1]

The second, already mentioned in the previous chapter, is exactly that text from *De Civitate Dei* in which the full legitimacy of spiritual interpretations is affirmed, provided that the historicity (i.e., reality) of the events reported in the holy books of the Old and New Testaments is not denied:

> No one, then, forbids us to understand Paradise according to these, and perhaps other, more appropriate, allegorical interpretations, while also believing in the truth of that story as presented to us in a most faithful narrative of events.[2]

Relying on these two Augustinian texts, Saint Thomas Aquinas will reformulate the same principle in his own manner, choosing the clearest possible terms:

---

[1] Augustine, *On Genesis*, introduction, translation and notes by Edmund Hill O.P. (New York: New City Press, 2002), 346.

[2] Supra, p. 11, n. 5.

> For whatever Scripture tells us about paradise is set down as matter of history; and wherever Scripture makes use of this method, we must hold to the historical truth [*veritas historiae*] of the narrative as a foundation of whatever spiritual explanation we may offer.[3]

The expression *veritas historiae* ("historical truth") used by its author has a distinct and very special signification. As if he anticipated the undermining of the traditional exegesis of the Bible intended both by historical-critical method specialists and by all those interpreters who speak of the "myths" of the two Testaments, Saint Thomas posits the unique, solid foundation for any possible interpretation: the historical truth of the events reported in the sacred texts. Situated in this most excellent hermeneutical tradition, Dominican Father Thomas Crean emphasizes that "the historical truth must be retained as the basis, and

[3] *The Summa Theologica of Saint Thomas Aquinas*, Translated by the Fathers of the English Dominican Province, Revised by Daniel J. Sullivan, available online on the New Advent website: https://www.newadvent.org/summa/1102.htm, "Ea enim quae de Paradiso in Scriptura dicuntur, per modum narrationis historicae proponuntur, in omnibus autem quae sic Scriptura tradit, est pro fundamento tenenda veritas historiae, et de super spirituales expositiones fabricandae." I quote the Latin text from the definitive edition established by Pope Leo XIII: Tomus Quintus, Pars Prima *Summa Theologiae* (Rome, 1889), 448.

spiritual interpretation built upon it."[4] Later on, he adds the following:

> Since the principal author of Holy Scripture is God Himself, the first Truth, it follows that where there is no indication in the text that a passage which seems to be historical is anything other than historical, then it should be taken according to its obvious sense.

Failure to adhere to this principle renders any interpretation trivial. At the same time, however, as we have already noted, positing historical veracity can have unexpected and undesirable consequences. Let us see what this entails.

Once the historical foundation of the biblical account regarding the location and nature of Paradise accounted in the Bible is established, Saint Thomas has to answer to a major objection already raised in his time. The objection in question starts from a practical, empirical finding based on numerous testimonies that do not *practically* confirm the existence of the terrestrial Paradise. For no one had ever found a place on earth that could have been said to shelter Paradise:

[4] Thomas Crean, O.P., "The Perfection of our First Parents, According to St Thomas Aquinas" (January 28, 2016): accessed November 10, 2025, https://kolbecenter.org/perfection-first-parents-aquinas/.

> Although men have explored the entire habitable world, yet none have made mention of the place of paradise. Therefore apparently it is not a corporeal place.[5]

To this objection, which anticipates the rejection of the existence of a historical Paradise by modern exegetes—like the (in)famous Rudolf Bultmann—eager to apply the so-called "demythologization" to the Holy Scripture, Saint Thomas Aquinas responds with remarkable firmness:

> The situation of paradise is shut off from the habitable world by mountains, or seas, or some torrid region, which cannot be crossed; and so people who have written about topography make no mention of it.[6]

No doubt can overshadow the firm conviction that results from following, with faithfulness, the principle of Saint Augustine's hermeneutics: both at

---

[5] *The Summa Theologica of Saint Thomas Aquinas*, Translated by the Fathers of the English Dominican Province, Revised by Daniel J. Sullivan, available online on the New Advent website: https://www.newadvent.org/summa/1102.htm, "Aliqui diligentissime inquisierunt omnia loca terrae habitabilis, qui tamen nullam mentionem faciunt de loco Paradisi. Ergo non videtur esse locus corporeus." Pars Prima, q. 102 a. 1 arg. 3, 448.

[6] *The Summa Theologica of Saint Thomas Aquinas*, "Ad tertium dicendum quod locus ille seclusus est a nostra habitatione aliquibus impedimentis vel montium, vel marium, vel alicuius aestuosae regionis, quae per transiri non potest. Et ideo scriptores locorum de hoc loco mentionem non fecerunt." Pars Prima, q. 102 a. 1 ad 3, 449.

the beginning of the creation and in the present, Paradise is truly situated somewhere in this world, in a physical location that is physically inaccessible. Shortly speaking, Paradise *is* real. Paradise *is* historical. If we read and reread these theological teachings and metaphysical speculations carefully, we will begin to discern the profound echo they cast on the writings of Christopher Columbus, where the Genoese navigator debates the same subject: the establishment of a terrestrial location, inaccessible yet locatable here in our fallen world, of the garden where the ancestors of humankind, Adam and Eve, were tempted by Satan.

To prove one more time that the Angelic Doctor never hesitates in his belief that Paradise is somewhere here, in our world, I will quote the second article of question 102 from *Prima Pars*. Here, we find him engaged in an extensive discussion about the hypothetical equatorial placement of the Garden of Eden. While not a fervent defender of any specific location, he carefully reaffirms the necessity of postulating the terrestrial existence of Paradise:

> Those who say that paradise was on the equinoctial line are of opinion that such a situation is most temperate, on account of the unvarying equality of day and night; that it is never too cold there, because the sun is never too far off; and never too hot, because,

> although the sun passes over the heads of the inhabitants, it does not remain long in that position. However, Aristotle distinctly says that such a region is uninhabitable on account of the heat. This seems to be more probable; because, even those regions where the sun does not pass vertically overhead, are extremely hot on account of the mere proximity of the sun. But whatever be the truth of the matter, we must hold that paradise was situated in a most temperate situation, whether on the equator or elsewhere.[7]

Unlike any of the sacred authors mentioned above, we today know with certainty that there is no inaccessible place on Earth—indeed, starting from the Renaissance period, it has been completely explored. Thus, Paradise is truly not hidden anywhere in the geography of the world accessible to

[7] *The Summa Theologica of Saint Thomas Aquinas*, "Ad quartum dicendum quod illi qui dicunt Paradisum esse sub circulo aequinoctiali, opinantur sub circulo illo esse locum temperatissimum, propter aequalitatem dierum et noctium omni tempore; et quia sol nunquam multum ab eis elongatur, ut sit apud eos superabundantia frigoris; nec iterum est apud eos, ut dicunt, superabundantia caloris, quia etsi sol pertranseat super eorum capita, non tamen diu moratur ibi in hac dispositione. Aristoteles tamen, in libro Meteor., expresse dicit quod regio illa est inhabitabilis propter aestum. Quod videtur probabilius, quia terrae per quas nunquam sol pertransit in directum capitis, sunt intemperatae in calore propter solam vicinitatem solis. Quidquid autem de hoc sit, credendum est Paradisum in loco temperatissimo constitutum esse, vel sub aequinoctiali vel alibi." Pars Prima, q. 102 a. 2 ad 4 A, 450.

us. Such a statement seems to contradict the beliefs of many Christians who lived in different eras: Saint Augustine, Saint Thomas Aquinas, and Christopher Columbus. Could they all have been mistaken? From a certain point of view, strictly geographical and naturalistic, yes; from a spiritual point of view and which takes into account the two states of world history – pre-lapsarian and post-lapsarian – no. What we must clarify, with great care, convinced by the empirical truth of the absence of an inaccessible geographic location on this Earth, is the difference between the world before the Fall and the world after the sin and exile of Adam and Eve in human history. The direction of a certain historical spiritual interpretation of the existence of Paradise is the path followed by both the mentioned authors and other brilliant Christian thinkers whom we will encounter in the following chapters. Their path is one that we ourselves must tread with both confidence and careful consideration.

CHAPTER 4

Columbus's Pear

Briefly presenting the opinions of the most influential Christian theologians and philosophers throughout the history of universal culture, Saints Augustine and Thomas Aquinas, I was able to identify the exact same type of interpretation that guided Columbus in his reflections on the location of Paradise. Before directing my attention to those fathers of the church who, I believe, correctly sketched the "map" that will help us reach the goal of our journey, I will return to the Genoese explorer and his interpretation regarding the location of Paradise. This time, the key text is found in his correspondence.

Although he does not cite the two saints in his letter to Their Royal Highnesses, Ferdinand and Isabella, he explicitly mentions the name of that giant of the first Christian millennium who conveyed to posterity the details of the literal, historical interpretation of Paradise: Saint Isidore of

Seville. In his phenomenal encyclopedic synthesis called *Etymologiae*,[1] he describes in the fourteenth book the location and nature of Paradise in terms that would later be used by Saint Thomas Aquinas in the texts I previously mentioned. Saint Isidore's exposition, naive and yet so picturesque, deserves to be quoted in its entirety:

> Paradise is located in the east. Its name, translated from Greek into Latin, means "garden." In Hebrew in turn it is called Eden, which in our language means "delights." The combination of both names gives us the expression "garden of delights," for every kind of fruit-tree and non-fruit bearing tree is found in this place, including the Tree of Life. It does not grow cold or hot there, but the air is always temperate. A spring which bursts forth in the center irrigates the whole grove and it is divided into the headwaters of four rivers. Access to this location was blocked off after the fall of humankind, for it is fenced in on all sides by a flaming sword, that is, encircled by a wall of fire, so that the flames almost reach the sky. Also the

[1] We might almost say, without error, that the *Etymologies* of Saint Isidore of Seville were for the whole of the Middle Ages and for the centuries that followed the equivalent of the *Larousse Dictionary* or the *Encyclopaedia Britannica*. From theology, history and philosophy, to anatomy, zoology, architecture, culinary art and architecture, there is no field of knowledge that has not been addressed by the Hispano-Roman doctor of the church.

> Cherubim, that is, a garrison of angels, have been drawn up above the flaming sword to prevent evil spirits from approaching, so that the flames drive off human beings, and angels drive off the wicked angels, in order that access to Paradise may not lie open either to flesh or to spirits that have transgressed.[2]

Let's summarize a few essential points captured in Saint Isidore of Seville's description: after the fall of the ancestors of the human race, Adam and Eve, access to Paradise is restricted; the forbidden garden is located in the East (which is why the text is included in the section of his encyclopedia titled

[2] Stephen A. Barney et al., eds., *The Etymologies of Isidore of Seville* (Cambridge University Press, 2006), 285–86. Here is the original text: "Paradisus est locus in orientis partibus constitutus, cuius vocabulum ex Graeco in Latinum vertitur hortus: porro Hebraice Eden dicitur, quod in nostra lingua deliciae interpretatur. Quod utrumque iunctum facit hortum deliciarum; est enim omni genere ligni et pomiferarum arborum consitus, habens etiam et lignum vitae: non ibi frigus, non aestus, sed perpetua veris temperies. E cujus medio fons prorumpens totum nemus irrigat, dividiturque in quattuor nascentia flumina, cujus loci post peccatum hominis aditus interclusus est. Septus est enim undique romphea flamma, id est muro igneo accinctus, ita ut ejus cum caelo pene jungatur incendium. Cherubin quoque, id est, angelorum praesidium arcendis spiritibus malis super rompheae flagrantiam ordinatum est, ut homines flammae, angelos vero malos angeli submoveant, ne cui carni, vel spiritui transgressionis aditus Paradisi pateat." Isidori Hispalensis Episcopi, *Opera Omnia*, Tomus IV, Etymologiarum, Libri X. posteriores (Rome, 1850), 143–44.

"Asia"); the climate is temperate; people are prevented from entering Paradise by a wall of fire; any attempts by fallen angels to return here are repelled by cherubim.

Among all these details, Saint Thomas Aquinas also mentioned, with some reservation, the theme of the wall of fire as well as the eastern location. However, in Christopher Columbus's accounts, we find almost *all* the details of Saint Isidore.

Before we see how these appear in Columbus's descriptions, I emphasize once again his unwavering conviction regarding the presence of the "garden of delights" in our world, subject to the vicissitudes and whims of history. It is precisely this conviction that compels Columbus to articulate a picture in which all, absolutely all, details confirm his formidable observation, dated August 17, 1498, and reported by Father Bartolomé de las Casas:

> That land from whence he came is a vast mainland, *or where the Earthly Paradise is.*[3]

Convinced that he had discovered unknown territories of the Indies, Columbus unhesitatingly assimilates the geography lesson of the learned man from Seville, who claims that Paradise is

[3] Olson and Bourne, *The Northmen*, 364–65. Emphasis added.

in Asia—therefore somewhere in the East.[4] The recording of climatic changes also indicates, through moderate temperatures following days of terrible heat, the proximity of Paradise. Likewise, the presence of abundant waters seems to indicate the source of the four rivers mentioned in the Genesis text. All these transform Columbus's suppositions into an irrefutable conviction:

> There are great indications of this being the terrestrial paradise, for its site coincides with the opinion of the holy and wise theologians whom I have mentioned; and moreover, the other evidences agree with the supposition, for I have never either read or heard of fresh water coming in so large a quantity, in close conjunction with the water of the sea; the idea is also corroborated by the blandness of the temperature; and if the water of which I speak, does not proceed from the earthly paradise, it appears to be still more marvelous, for I do not believe that there is any river in the world so large or so deep.[5]

[4] In the letter to the Catholic Monarchs he insists on this geographical positioning. "Saints Isidore and Bede, Strabo, and the master of scholastic history (i.e., Petrus Comestor), with Saint Ambrose, Scotus, and all learned theologians, agree that the earthly paradise is in the east." *Select Letters of Cristopher Columbus, with Original Documents, relating to his Four Voyages to the New World* (London, 1847), 136.

[5] *Select Letters*, 137–38.

The only thing missing from Columbus's letter is the wall of fire mentioned by Saint Isidore. Once this fact is noted, it is natural to ask: How then is the access of the unworthy creatures—fallen men or angels—prevented in Paradise? The answer is quite simple: by altitude. In other words, the height at which it is located makes access impossible for any person or vehicle. For Paradise, asserts Columbus, is situated on the summit of a mountain. However, not a sharp mountain that proudly soars towards the sky, but a flattened mountain, shaped like the flesh of a pear:

> I do not suppose that the earthly paradise is in the form of a rugged mountain, as the descriptions of it have made it appear, but that it is on the summit of the spot, which I have described as being in the form of the stalk of a pear; the approach to it from a distance must be by a constant and gradual ascent; but I believe that, as I have already said, no one could ever reach the top.[6]

As we can see in most studies dedicated to Columbus, the pear shape of the world has elicited numerous ironic reactions. Until now, however, I have not encountered a satisfactory explanation of *the logic* that led to such a vision. This logic derives

[6] Ibid., 137.

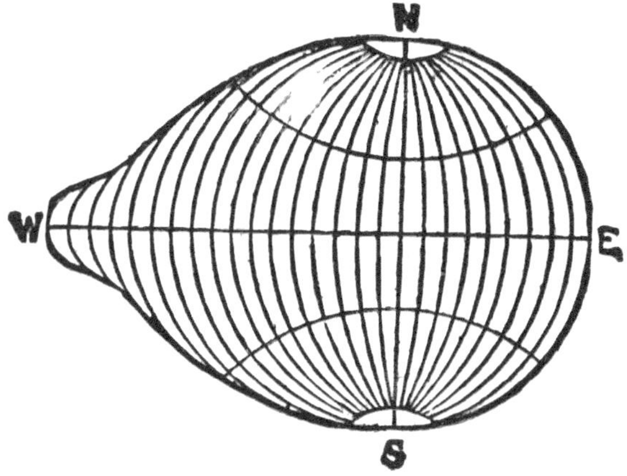

The pear-shaped Earth of Columbus. (From *Paradise Found*, William Fairfield Warren, 1885.)

directly from the author's unwavering belief that Paradise truly exists, as unanimously asserted by Saints Augustine, Isidore of Seville, and Thomas Aquinas, somewhere in our fallen world. But what does this have to do with the pear shape of the world? Only in this way can the survival of humanity's original homeland, after the Great Flood, be explained. Without this mountain, the floodwaters would have forever submerged the garden that shelters the Tree of Life described both in the first book of the Holy Scriptures, Genesis, and the last, the Revelation of Saint John. This is why Columbus's world must have such a strange shape. Therefore, not an egg, as suggested by the well-known expression "the egg of Columbus," but a pear.

A shape dictated, certainly, by the postulate of the historical existence of Paradise, which Columbus defends even at the cost of sacrificing complete fidelity to the biblical text—like Saint Thomas Aquinas—that clearly states that during the flood "the waters rose and covered the mountains to a depth of more than fifteen cubits" (Genesis 7:20). For the navigator, the primary motivation is particularly practical: he strives to prove to Their Royal Highnesses the immense significance of his expeditions, which, for this reason, must continue to be generously supported. In the case of the mentioned saintly doctors, however, the situation is not as dramatic. On the contrary, they never forget the true significance of the postulate of the historical existence of Paradise. But this significance, as we shall see, lies in the spiritual—i.e., allegorical-symbolic—interpretation of Paradise.

CHAPTER 5

Reopening the Gates of Heaven

One of the smaller yet no less profound works left as a legacy by Saint Thomas Aquinas is the so-called *Expositio in Symbolum Apostolorum* (*On the Apostles' Creed*).[1] As the title indicates, we are dealing with a series of lessons (i.e., catechesis) intended for the Christian people, lessons that the Angelic Doctor himself probably presented either in the squares of various Italian cities or in the churches of the parishes where he was invited to preach. All these teachings were based on the Apostles' Creed—the miniature synthesis of the Christian faith.

The large number of preserved editions demonstrates the popularity of these extremely simple and

[1] I use the English translation by Joseph B. Collins and published in 1939. For the Latin text I quote the edition from the Corpus Thomisticum reference website: http://www.corpusthomisticum.org/csv.html.

penetrating texts, in which Saint Thomas's genius presented itself before the astonished crowds. Thus, commenting on the fourth article of the Creed, the one that tells us about the Savior Christ that "he suffered under Pontius Pilate, was crucified, died, and was buried," the commentator offers us some appropriate answers to a crucial question:

> But what need was there that the Son of God should suffer for us? There was a great need; and indeed it can be assigned to two reasons. The first is that it was a remedy against sin, and the second is for an example of what we ought to do.[2]

Subsequently, he will show, in his usual systematic manner, that there are five different kinds of evils into which man falls through his own sins, evils that could only be removed by the sacrifice of the second person of the Holy Trinity, Jesus Christ, the Incarnate Word. The fifth evil that affects sinful man particularly interests us in the context of our historical, philosophical and theological inquiry regarding Paradise:

---

[2] Thomas Aquinas, *On the Apostles' Creed*, trans. Joseph B. Collins (n.p., 1939), 28. The Latin text: "Sed quae necessitas ut verbum Dei pateretur pro nobis? Magna: et potest colligi duplex necessitas. Una est ad remedium contra peccata, alia est ad exemplum quantum ad agenda." Thomae de Aquino, *Expositio in Symbolum Apostolorum*: accessed November 10, 2025, http://www.corpusthomisticum.org/csv.html.

Fifthly, we incur banishment from the kingdom of heaven. Those who offend kings are compelled to go into exile. Thus, man is expelled from heaven on account of sin. Adam was driven out of paradise immediately after his sin, and the gate of paradise was shut. But Christ by His sufferings and death opened this gate and recalled all the exiles to the kingdom. *With the opening of the side of Christ, the gate of Paradise is opened*; and with the pouring out of His blood, guilt is washed away, satisfaction is made to God, infirmity is removed, punishment is expiated, and the exiles are called back to the kingdom. Hence, the thief received the immediate response: "This day you shall be with Me in Paradise" [Luke 23:43]. Never before was this spoken to anyone, not to Adam, not to Abraham, not to David; but this day [i.e., as soon as the gate is opened] the thief, having asked for pardon, received it: "Having a confidence in the entering into the holies by the blood of Christ" [Hebrews 10:19]. From all this then is seen the effect of the passion of Christ as a remedy for sin.[3]

[3] *On the Apostles' Creed*, 28. Emphasis added. "Quinto in currimus exilium regni. Nam qui offendunt reges, exula recoguntur a regno. Sic et homo propter peccatum expellitur de Paradiso. Inde est quod Adam statim post peccatum est eiectus de Paradiso, et clausa est ianua Paradisi. Sed Christus sua passione ianuam illam aperuit, et ad regnum exules revocavit. Aperto enim latere Christi, aperta est ianua Paradisi; et fuso sanguine eius, deleta est macula, placatus est Deus, ablata est debilitas, expiata est poena, exules revocantur ad regnum. Et inde est quod statim latroni dicitur (Luc.

From what we learn from Saint Thomas Aquinas's commentary, we recognize the biblical passage that is implicitly mentioned. It is from the Gospel of John, chapter 19, verse 34:

> But one of the soldiers with a spear opened his side, and immediately there came out blood and water.

Drawing on the account of the apostle John, the Angelic Doctor develops a fascinating interpretation regarding *how* it is possible to re-enter in to the lost Paradise. Firstly, he precisely identifies the cardinal moment of reopening the access to the world of eternal life: when the side of Jesus Christ was opened with a spear. At the same time, he astonishes us with the nature of his interpretation. After seeing in the *Summa Theologiae* that he attributes a major importance to the historical, i.e., geographical existence of the Garden of Eden, it now seems that we are suddenly faced with a spiritual interpretation that raises additional questions.

For how can we concretely see the gate of heaven in the opening of the Savior Christ's side from which

XXIII, 43): hodie mecum eris in Paradiso. Hoc non est dictum olim: non enim dictum fuit alicui, non Adae, non Abrahae, non David; sed hodie, scilicet quando aperta est ianua, latro veniam petit et invenit. Hebr. X, 19: habentes (. . .) fiduciam in introitu sanctorum in sanguine Christi. Sic ergo patet utilitas ex parte remedii." *Expositio in Symbolum Apostolorum.*

blood and water flow? What subtle and invisible connection does such a moment of the Passion of Our Lord, Jesus Christ, have with the issue of the location of Paradise? Moreover, as if these questions were not enough, there is also the relationship between death—understood as departure from the physical, visible world—and access to heaven: Is this correlation inevitable? Does this mean that Paradise is accessible only *through* and *beyond* death? All these questions only increase the mystery. We might smile imagining Admiral Christopher Columbus—engaged in the conquest of terrestrial Paradise—grappling with the series of interrogations prompted by the Angelic Doctor's allegoric interpretation.

To elucidate the mystery, I will follow the most natural course of any historical investigation. I will begin by examining the sources of Saint Thomas's interpretation, especially the Gospel of Saint John in that amazing translation realized by Saint Jerome: *Biblia Sacra Vulgata*—the reference version of the Roman Catholic Church. Here, translated into Latin, verse 34 of chapter 19 of the Gospel of John reads:

> Sed unus militum lancea latus ejus aperuit,
> et continuo exivit sanguis et aqua.[4]

[4] *Biblia Sacra Juxtam Vulgatam Clementinam*, Plurimis Consultis Editionibus Diligenter Praeparata a Michaele Tvveedale, MMXVII (Baronius, 2017), 132. For the Latin version of the Holy Scriptures I will use this edition.

The Douay-Rheims translation is unequivocal:

> But one of the soldiers with a spear opened his side, and immediately there came out blood and water.

It is this extremely precious nuance that speaks of *the opening* (not *the piercing*) of the side of the Divine Savior that triggers Saint Thomas's interpretation. He will connect this passage with the first verse of chapter 4 of Revelation, where we also find the image of an open door in heaven:

> It deserves notice that he does not say wounded but pierced, that is opened, because in his side the door of eternal life is opened to us: After this I looked, and lo, in heaven, an open door! [Revelation 4:1]. This is the door in the side of the ark through which those animals entered who were not to perish in the flood [Genesis 7]. This door is the cause of our salvation; and so, at once there came out blood and water. This is a remarkable miracle—that blood should flow from the body of a dead person where blood congeals.[5]

[5] Saint Thomas Aquinas, *Commentary on the Gospel of Saint John*, Translated by James A. Weisheipl, O.P., and Fabian R. Larcher, O.P., Chapter 19, Lecture 5: https://isidore.co/aquinas/John19.htm. The Latin text is also provided here in parallel: "Et signanter dicit aperuit, non vulneravit; quia per hoc latus, aperitur nobis ostium vitae aeternae. Apoc. IV, 1: post hoc vidi ostium apertum. Hoc est ostium in latere arcae, per quod intrant animalia

Although extremely concise, lacking any literary embellishments, the Thomistic commentary contains a set of ideas similar to those in Saint Jerome's interpretation that underpinned his epochal translation. The first of these ideas clearly arises from the use of the verb *aperīre* (to open) in Latin, instead of the Greek ἔνυξεν ("*enyxen*"—to wound or pierce), as found in the Greek version of the Gospel of John. This detail prevented the full manifestation of the hermeneutic enthusiasm of some great Greek doctors like Saint John Chrysostom, who, although he speaks like Saint Thomas about the sacramental and ecclesial significance of the blood and water that flowed from the side pierced by the Roman soldier's spear, does not mention the opening of the gates of Paradise.[6] Additionally, the connections made with the text from the book of Revelation allow us to glimpse an entire vision of history whose texture merits thorough investigation. For us, however, what is relevant is recognizing all the key ideas in Saint Thomas's interpretation (which, by the way,

diluvio non peritura: Gen. VII. Sed hoc ostium est causa salutis, unde continuo exivit sanguis et aqua, quod est valde miraculosum, ut de corpore mortui, in quo est congelatus sanguis, sanguis exeat." https://isidore.co/aquinas/John19.htm.

[6] *Homilies of Saint John Chrysostom on the Gospel of John* (Oxford, 1852), 761. The text can be read online here: http://www.newadvent.org/fathers/240185.htm.

do not belong to him. They first were developed and made manifest in Saint Augustine's commentary on the Gospel of John):

> A suggestive word was made use of by the evangelist, in not saying *pierced*, or *wounded* His side, or anything else, but *opened*; that thereby, in a sense, the gate of life might be thrown open, from whence have flowed forth the sacraments of the Church, without which there is no entrance to the life which is the true life. That blood was shed for the remission of sins; that water it is that makes up the health-giving cup, and supplies at once the laver of baptism and water for drinking. This was announced beforehand, when Noah was commanded to make a door in the side of the ark [Genesis 6:16], whereby the animals might enter which were not destined to perish in the flood, and by which the Church was prefigured.[7]

[7] Augustine, [*Tractates (Lectures) on the Gospel of John*], trans. John Gibb, in *Nicene and Post-Nicene Fathers*, ed. Philip Schaff, First Series, vol. 7 (Buffalo, NY: Christian Literature Publishing, 1888). The text can be read online here: https://www.newadvent.org/fathers/1701120.htm. "Vigilanti verbo Evangelista usus est, ut non diceret: *Latus eius percussit,* aut *vulneravit*, aut quid aliud; sed, aperuit: ut illic quodammodo vitae ostium panderetur, unde Sacramenta Ecclesiae manaverunt, sine quibus ad vitam quae vera vita est, non intratur. Ille sanguis in remissionem fusus est peccatorum: aqua illa salutare temperat poculum; haec et lavacrum praestat, et potum. Hoc praenuntiabat quod Noe in latere arcae ostium facere iussus est, qua intrarent animalia quae non erant diluvi operitura, quibus praefigurabatur Ecclesia." *Patrologia Latina*, 41, 1953. The

Later, in the fifteenth book of his final monumental work and theological synthesis, *De Civitate Dei*, Augustine will revisit the typological-allegorical interpretation applied to Noah's Ark, emphasizing the significance of each detail in the body of that marvelous construction. When he reaches the door provided in the side of the Ark—understood in connection with the gates of heaven reopened when the side of our Lord, Jesus Christ, was opened—Saint Augustine conclusively restates the same allegorical interpretation proposed in his commentary on the Gospel of John:

> And its having a door made in the side of it certainly signified the wound which was made when the side of the Crucified was pierced with the spear; for by this those who come to Him enter; for thence flowed the sacraments by which those who believe are initiated.[8]

For both Saint Augustine and his devoted reader, Thomas Aquinas, the reopening of the gates of

original Latin text can also be read online on the official website dedicated to Saint Augustine: https://www.augustinus.it/latino/commento_vsg/omelia_120_testo.htm.

[8] Saint Augustine, *The City of God against the Pagans*, trans. Robert W. Dyson (Cambridge University Press, 1998), 687. "Et quod ostium in latere accepit, profecto illud est uulnus, quando latus crucifixi lancea perforatum est; hac quippe ad illum uenientes ingrediuntur, quia inde sacramenta manarunt, quibus credentes initiantur." *Patrologia Latina*, 1845, 41, 472.

Heaven is an unparalleled event signified by the opening of the side of the Savior Jesus Christ crucified on the cross. Water, a fundamental symbol of holy baptism, and blood, the essential symbol of the Holy Eucharist, represent the foundation of religious life that, lived consistently according to Christian faith, guides all who embrace it in heaven. The Church Militant (*ecclesia militans*) present here, in this earthly life, in the fires of trials and persecutions triggered by a hostile world, represents the outpost of heaven, of the "Jerusalem above." Membership in the church through baptism is synonymous with a genuine "return to Paradise." For all church fathers and doctors, the ecclesiastical institution, in its original sense, is nothing other than the "terrestrial Paradise" once lost by Adam and Eve through the original sin committed in Eden.

This seems to be a substantial allegorical response to the question raised by Horia-Roman Patapievici in the essay "Where Has Paradise Gone?" Yet, we cannot avoid the discussion on the historical location of Paradise conducted by Saints Augustine, Isidore, and Thomas in their works. As we have already seen, they postulate the geographical existence—in a location protected by mountains, water, or extreme heat—of the lost garden that is hidden from us. Inevitably, this apparent contradiction confronts us, much like the very wall of fire mentioned by Saint Isidore of Seville, in the form of a question still unanswered: How does this understanding, based on a strictly *literal* and *historical* (and even *geographical*) reading of the sacred texts, reconcile with the Augustinian *spiritual-allegorical* interpretation? If we were to broaden the mystery and deepen our own astonishment, we might derive other equally difficult questions: for instance, how is it possible for a baptized member of the church here on earth to also be a member of the kingdom of heaven situated in the "unseen world"? How is it possible to be simultaneously in two different locations, *here* and *there*?

Unlike Saints Augustine and Thomas Aquinas, as well as Admiral Christopher Columbus, we must recognize that we have a considerable advantage: due to research and explorations over the last centuries, today, at least, we are certain that there is no inaccessible location on earth that conceals Eden. It is precisely this that has directed my research in the only direction that allowed me to reveal the most plausible answer. To unveil it, however, we will need to change our path: if initially, we started from Columbus's strictly geographical search towards the theological and historical interpretations that motivated it, it is now time to address, directly, the text of Genesis to extract all those ideas that can lead us to the goal: a goal that is not only Columbus's but also ours, as Christian believers of the twenty-first century. The allegorical-spiritual interpretation developed by Saints Augustine and Thomas Aquinas has already guided us in the right direction.

CHAPTER 6

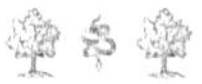

Saint Gregory of Nyssa, Saint Gregory of Nazianzus, and the Two Trees from Eden

The fervor for exploration and travel over the past five centuries has grown exponentially. Adventurers, scholars, journalists, and mere curious individuals have ceaselessly traversed every corner of the Earth. Even though there are still hard-to-reach regions, such as the Tibetan Plateau, the Himalayas, or certain areas of Papua New Guinea, we can be certain that no place on the face of the Earth has remained unexplored. Even the depths of the oceans have been the target of divers and submarines that have descended into the abyss of the Mariana Trench. Over one thousand and three hundred years after Saint Isidore composed his *Etymologies* and more than nine centuries after Saint Thomas Aquinas wrote *Summa Theologiae*, we know that, besides the invaluable insights provided by their work guided by eternal wisdom, in a certain respect they were mistaken: the lost Paradise is not found, surrounded by a huge wall of fire or protected by some inaccessible height, here on Earth. Christopher Columbus, convinced he had traversed the region close to the garden of eternal life, was the victim of an optical error corrected through the comprehensive, exhaustive exploration of the entire Earth.

To those who are quick to conclude that the history recounted in the first chapters of Genesis is a mere "myth," I hasten to respond: The establishment of the non-existence of the hypothetical terrestrial location of Paradise in no way means denying its historical reality. Adam and Eve truly existed, as did the tree of knowledge and the trickster serpent. However, the *ontological nature* of their existence, or more cautiously said, *the quality* (i.e., *the glory*) of their life before original sin was much different from what we, their descendants, experience now. Understanding these things requires patience and a certain effort of comprehension. Obtaining complete and accurate answers to all the key questions about the pre-lapsarian world of the first humans is not an easy task.

Our only significant advantage is access to all the writings of those saints, doctors, and mystics of the Christian Tradition, who have left us interpretations that elucidate, as much as possible, the mystery of Eden's historical existence. Before continuing our journey, let's list all those questions whose answers will allow us to obtain a clear and well-defined picture:

What is the Tree of Life and the tree of the knowledge of good and evil? What about the forbidden fruit? What is the profound nature of original sin? Who or what is the serpent? And what are the "garments of skins" (Genesis 3:21) with which God himself endowed the progenitors after the sin? What does the "flaming sword, turning every way" (Genesis 3:24), with which the cherubim prevent our access to Paradise, represent?

First, I will address the first three questions from the list above, questions that, in essence, indicate the related aspects of the same issue. To eliminate, from the outset, certain interpretations that are as persuasive as they are superficial, I will emphasize that the biblical account does not match the famous fairy tale by the Grimm brothers, "Snow White." Adam and Eve did not bite into an apple.

A defender and proponent of a spiritual-symbolic (i.e., allegorical) interpretation embraced by many of the most brilliant saints and doctors of the church, Saint Gregory of Nyssa opens the doors to a vision whose depth cannot be fully grasped in our current condition. Despite the inherent limitations of our fallen state, the speculations of the subtle saint from Cappadocia provide, much like the interpretations of Saint Augustine, several points supporting the imperative necessity of the symbolic interpretation of the Bible.

First of all, he recalls the famous verse of Saint Paul: "the letter killeth, but the spirit quickeneth" (2 Corinthians 3:6). Following this axiom, he emphasizes that "frequently the narrative, if we stop short at the mere events, does not furnish us with models of the good life. How does it profit the cause of a virtuous life to hear that the prophet Hosea got himself a child by sexual malfeasance (Hosea 1:2) and that Isaiah went in to the prophetess (Isaiah 8:3), if one stops short at the literal sense? Or what do the stories about David, in which adultery and murder have agreed together in a single crime (cf. 2 Kings 11), contribute to the virtuous life?"[1] However, all these interpretative directions are revealed after Gregory of Nyssa mentions, like Saint Augustine, Saint Paul's interpretation in the

[1] Gregory of Nyssa, *Homilies on the Song of Songs*, trans. Richard A. Norris, Jr. (Atlanta: Society of Biblical Literature, 2012), 5, 7.

fourth chapter of the Epistle to the Galatians where "recalling the two sons of Abraham born to him by a slave woman and by a free woman, he calls their interpretation allegory." The purpose of these rhetorical questions is to demonstrate the correctness of the allegorical interpretation, which is not only possible but in certain biblical contexts becomes imperatively necessary. To prove its legitimacy, he states that "after he has mentioned the two sons of Abraham, born to him of the maidservant and the free woman, Paul designates his way of understanding them an 'allegory'" (Galatians 4:24).[2] Therefore, there is a biblical basis for allegorical interpretation that cannot be ignored.

God Himself, through the sacred texts of which He is the Author, has willed to propose this form of interpretation to help us detach from the "bodily" meanings of the holy writings. Finally, last but not least, he mentions "countless instances of this sort of thing to be gathered from the sayings in the Gospels, instances in which one thing is conveyed by the obvious sense but something else is indicated by the intelligible meaning of what is said."[3] Some examples: the water that Christ promised to the thirsty, through which believers become springs of flowing

[2] Ibid.

[3] Ibid.

waters (John 7:37–38); or the bread that comes down from heaven (John 6:50–51); the temple that is destroyed and raised up in three days (John 2:19); the way (John 14:6); the door (John 10:9); the stone that is rejected by the builders and is fitted in as the chief cornerstone (Mark 12:10); two persons upon a single bed (Luke 17:34); the two women grinding at the mill, one of whom is taken and the other left (Matthew 24:41); the corpse and the eagles (Matthew 24:28); the fig tree that becomes tender and puts forth its leaves (Matthew 24:32).

Seeking the spiritual meanings of sacred texts does not mean, according to Saint Gregory of Nyssa, anything other than moving from the literal sense, which contains non-rational or irrational aspects, to a spiritual, rational understanding, accessible to those advancing towards "a perfect man, unto the measure of the age of the fullness of Christ" (Ephesians 4:13).

All texts that require a spiritual, allegorical interpretation contain elements that, at first glance, seem irrational. These elements, however, once grasped, allow us to see—by contrast—the rational significance (i.e., in accordance with the divine Logos) of the respective texts. To make my statements as clear as possible, I will propose two examples, among the most well known.

Any Christian has heard countless times the famous parable of the sower. Retold by the evangelist Matthew (chapter 13) and Mark (chapter 4) and Luke (chapter 8), the parable recounts, among other things, an improbable event that provokes spontaneous questions: What sower would throw seeds on a stone? Or among thorns? Any farmer would probably explain to us, perhaps smiling embarrassedly, that the land is carefully prepared and the seeds are planted under optimal conditions. They would never be thrown into those places mentioned by Christ in His parable. For a farmer, such behavior would be irrational. And, of course, the farmer is right. But God did not incarnate to teach us agriculture. Not at all. He came to earth to teach us essential things so that we might re-enter, like the thief to the right of the crucified Savior Christ, Saint Dismas, into Paradise. Then what does He want to tell us through the parable of the sower, which contains, as we see, elements that can scandalize the reason of any decent farmer? Fortunately for us, the apostles asked Him, "What does this parable mean?" (Luke 8:9). He answered them:

> When any one heareth the word of the kingdom, and understandeth it not, there cometh the wicked one, and catcheth away that which was sown in his heart: this is he that received

> the seed by the way side. And he that received the seed upon stony ground, is he that heareth the word, and immediately receiveth it with joy. Yet hath he not root in himself, but is only for a time: and when there ariseth tribulation and persecution because of the word, he is presently scandalized. And he that received the seed among thorns, is he that heareth the word, and the care of this world and the deceitfulness of riches choketh up the word, and he becometh fruitless. But he that received the seed upon good ground, is he that heareth the word, and understandeth, and beareth fruit, and yieldeth the one an hundredfold, and another sixty, and another thirty. (Matthew 13:19–23)[4]

Behold! A spiritual, allegorical interpretation offered by our Lord Himself. An interpretation that clarifies the purpose of those statements presenting a sower who would throw his seeds on rocky ground or among thorns. In fact, through all of this, we are to understand the different types of "soil" on which the divine words were cast. Essentially, it is about the state of our hearts: we can have hearts of stone, of flesh, full of the weeds of sin, or, on the contrary, we can have hearts submissive to and open to the work of divine grace.

[4] *Biblia Sacra Juxtam Vulgatam Clementinam*, Plurimis Consultis Editionibus Diligenter Praeparata a Michaele Tvveedale, MMXVII (Baronius, 2017), 19–20.

Another such biblical sequence recounts a real-life episode whose protagonist was, again, our Savior. The Gospel according to Mark (11:12–14) tells us that, one day, Jesus became hungry. And, being hungry, He looked for fruit in a fig tree found by the roadside. Nothing more natural for those who have the privilege of living in villages blessed with orchards and fruit trees. However, the Savior found no fruit in that fig tree. This immediately attracted His tremendous wrath: He cursed the tree, which withered at once. The shock of the readers is amplified by a small detail related in the holy text of the Gospel: "For it was not the time for figs" (Mark 11:13). Instantly, the question arises: What rational person would be upset about not finding fruit in a tree whose fruiting season had not yet arrived? What rational person would seek fruit out of its specific season?

Our minds, intrigued by such an episode, must seek the answer. It seems that this is precisely what God, the divine author, desires: He wants us to ask questions. He wants us to seek the treasures hidden in the holy texts. In a word, He invites us, like pearl hunters, to dive into the deep waters of the Bible to seek the jewels hidden in the shells of His words. For He wants us to make a thorough effort to read and meditate on the holy texts. A perfect teacher, God knows that only in this way can our minds themselves—like the seashells – open to receive the rays of the light of grace, which God, as Saint Alphonsus Maria de Liguori tells us, does not wish to offer us except through prayer and asceticism. The asceticism of prayerful meditations, of assiduous readings, can provide us with the appropriate answer to such mysteries.

The cursed fig tree is a symbol of a reality of the same nature as that discussed in the parable of the sower: it is about us, people everywhere. *We* are the fig trees in which God, when He so wills, seeks fruit. Therefore, He does not wish to teach us about fruit trees, but about His expectations of us, Christians. But what fruits does He wish to find in our souls, in our hearts? I will leave you to answer that. I will do the same regarding the difficult question of the reasons that God speaks in parables and proposes allegorical interpretations to us.

Now, guided by Saint Gregory of Nyssa, we will address the text of Genesis from which we learn about the existence of the two trees in Paradise:

> And the Lord God brought forth of the ground all manner of trees, fair to behold, and pleasant to eat of: the Tree of Life also in the midst of paradise: and the tree of knowledge of good and evil. (Genesis 2: 9)[5]

[5] Ibid., 6. "Produxitque Dominus Deus de humo omne lignum pulchrum visu, et ad vescendum suave lignum etiam vitae in medio paradisi, lignumque scientiae boni et mali."

As we will see immediately, we are dealing with a geometric impossibility—a circle with two centers. However, Saint Gregory of Nyssa, who spent many years of his life studying the Holy Scripture alongside his brother, Saint Basil the Great, and his sister, Saint Macrina, immediately notices the anomaly. Here is what he states in his commentary on the Song of Songs:

> The tree of which it was forbidden to eat [Genesis 2:17] was not, as some have asserted, a fig tree or any other fruit bearing tree. For if the fig was a death-dealer in those days, it would not be perfectly edible now. We have at the same time learned this truth, in a negative form, from the voice of the Master, as it lays down the principle that none of the things that enter through the mouth is capable of defiling a person [Matthew 15:11]. Where that law [Genesis 2:17] is concerned, then, we look for some other meaning, and one that is worthy of the greatness of the Lawgiver. Even though we are informed that the garden is a product of divine husbandry and that the Tree of Life is planted in the middle of the garden, we want to learn from the Revealer of hidden mysteries what growths they are that the Father plants and tends and also how it is possible for there to be two trees right at the midpoint of the garden: the tree that saves and the tree that destroys. For the exact midpoint lies precisely

> at the one center, just as within the circumference of a circle. If, however, another center is set to one side of the center, it follows of necessity that the circle's position is shifted along with the center, with the result that the first center is no longer the midpoint. But if there was only a single garden in that place, how can the Word assert that each of the trees is to be treated of separately and yet say that both of them stand at the midpoint, even while the Word, in asserting that all the works of God are "very good" [Genesis 1:31], informs us that of the two trees the death-dealer has no place in the estate that God plants? Unless one perceives the truth in these matters through philosophy, what is being said will appear to the inattentive to be incoherent or mythical.[6]

The first statement is categorical: the Tree of Life and the tree of the knowledge of good and evil cannot be what they seem at first glance—simple fruit-bearing trees. To support his assertion, Saint Gregory cites several biblical texts that indicate the spiritual dimension of the act of eating. The essence is encapsulated in the following verse:

> Not in bread alone doth man live, but in every word that proceedeth from the mouth of God. (*Deuteronomy* 8:3)[7]

[6] Gregory of Nyssa, *Homilies*, 9.

[7] *Biblia Sacra Juxtam Vulgatam Clementinam*, 195.

This Old Testament text is referenced by Christ Himself when confronted with the temptation of hunger (Matthew 4:4). Here, the direction of an interpretation that transcends the literal text of scripture already begins to emerge. However, the decisive argument is provided by the detail regarding the placement of the two trees: how can the two trees be situated at the same central point of the garden? Saint Gregory of Nyssa's suggestion is clear. We are not dealing with two physical trees that have two distinct and irreducible entities, but with *a single reality* represented by the symbolic image of the two trees, a reality accessible in two different aspects.

In his commentary on Genesis, titled *De opificio hominis* (*On the Making of Man*), he explains the profound nature of the two trees. The first, the Tree of Life, is divine wisdom, about which the wise Solomon explicitly states in the book of Proverbs:

> She is a Tree of Life to them that lay hold on her: and he that shall retain her is blessed. (Proverbs 3:18)[8]

Saint Gregory of Nyssa hastens to add that Solomon actually "understands the Lord" under the

[8] Ibid., 677, "Lignum vitae est his qui apprehenderint eam, et qui tenuerit eam beatus."

name of Wisdom. And the Lord cannot be known better anywhere, as Saint Jerome shows us, than in Holy Scripture—the sum of His holy words. Through this interpretation, identifying the Tree of Life explicitly with God Himself and implicitly with the Holy Scripture, the path of exegesis is opened, reaching full maturity in the works of Saint Bonaventure. This learned follower of Saint Francis of Assisi will show that, in the context of the church, Holy Scripture can be, depending on how the holy text is understood, either the "Tree of Life" or the "tree of the knowledge of good and evil." Thus, one who knows the spiritual dimension of the sacred texts feeds from the Tree of Life, while one who limits himself to the knowledge of the letter eats from the tree of death.[9]

[9] Joseph Ratzinger, *The Theology of History in St. Bonaventure* (Chicago: Franciscan Herald Press, 1989), 151–52. Originally published as *Die Geschichtstheologie des heiligen Bonaventura* (Münich, 1959). The Bonaventurian text of reference is *Collationes in Hexaemeron*, composed of notes taken by his students during a series of 23 lectures given by the Franciscan general at the University of Paris in 1273, between the feast of Easter and that of Pentecost. In note 52 on page 236 of the English edition, Ratzinger states the following: "Unfortunately I was not able to determine the source for this interpretation. Most likely we would not be entirely wrong if we were to think of Joachim. But perhaps the history of the idea goes back further." I believe I can assert that Saints Gregory of Nyssa and Gregory of Nazianzus are very likely the main sources of this interpretative tradition. Of course, the complete lineage remains to be revealed by patristic scholars.

Returning to Saint Gregory of Nyssa's commentary from *De opificio hominis* regarding the second paradisiacal tree, the core of his commentary is found in his reflection on the notion of "knowledge." The text is so crucially important that I have decided to include all the main original Greek concepts in parentheses:

> What then is that which includes the knowledge of good and evil blended together, and is decked with the pleasures of sense? I think I am not aiming wide of the mark in employing, as a starting-point for my speculation, the sense of knowable [τῆς θεωρίας]. It is not, I think, science [ἐπιστήμην] which the Scripture here means by knowledge [γνῶσιν]; but I find a certain distinction, according to Scriptural use, between knowledge [γνώσεώς] and discernment [διακρίσεως]: for to discern scientifically [διακρίνειν ἐπιστημόνως] the good from the evil, the Apostle says is a mark of a more perfect condition and of exercised senses [Hebrews 1:14], for which reason also he bids us "prove all things" [1 Thessalonians 5:21], and says that discernment [τὸ διακρίνειν] belongs to the spiritual man [1 Corinthians 2:15] but knowledge [γνῶσις] is not always to be understood of skill [τὴν ἐπιστήμην] and acquaintance with anything, but of the disposition towards what is agreeable—as the "Lord knows them that are His" [2 Timothy 2:19]; and He says

> to Moses, "I knew you above all" [Exodus 33:12]; while of those condemned in their wickedness He Who knows all things says, "I never knew you" [Matthew 7:23].[10]

From this entire passage, several essential ideas emerge that encapsulate the essence of one of the most interesting interpretations ever given to the nature of the two trees in Paradise. First, the act of eating is equated with the act of knowing. Then, we receive the most subtle and powerful hint regarding what the two trees *are not*. For while we can say, even in a literal sense, that the fruit of any tree gives us life (in the sense that it helps us sustain our bodily life, which would be gravely endangered without food and water), about the fruit of which tree could we say that it gives us knowledge? We can eat any fruits we want—apples, pears, peaches, pineapples, bananas, etc.—and we will never gain the "knowledge of good and evil."

This suggests that the profound reality of what the holy text calls the "tree of the knowledge of good and evil" is different from that of any ordinary fruit tree. The two trees in Paradise are not

[10] Gregory of Nyssa, *De opificio hominis*, transl. H.A. Wilson, in *Nicene and Post-Nicene Fathers*, ed. Philip Schaff and Henry Wace, Second Series, vol. 5 (Buffalo, NY: Christian Literature Publishing, 1893). Available online here: https://www.newadvent.org/fathers/2914.htm.

ordinary trees, although the biblical image of the Fall caused by the act of eating a fruit remains perfectly valid for all of us, regardless of the subtlety of the reading we apply to the scriptures. However, the most important thing is that Saint Gregory of Nyssa opens the doors of understanding the nature of the two trees by directing our attention to the essential point: the very concept of "knowledge." This is the key that allows for the correct understanding of the Genesis text concerning the forbidden fruit and the fall of the protoparents Adam and Eve.

To take a step further, I will say that if the unique reality with which, by relating to it, would have given them life or death, the final result is the consequence of embracing a certain type of knowledge (γνῶσιν / gnōsin)—that of "good and evil," to the detriment of another type of knowledge (τὴν ἐπιστήμην / tēn epistēmēn) which would have allowed them to maintain the supernatural life of grace. Thus, the act of eating, so significant in its simplicity, indicates precisely this exercise of *a transformative knowledge*, as profound and special as in all those biblical verses quoted by the holy Cappadocian father: "The Lord knows those who are His" (2 Timothy 2:19); "I knew you above all" (Exodus 33:12); "I never knew you" (Matthew 7:23).

The difference between the two types of cognition, "knowledge" (Gr. γνώσεώς / gnōseōs / Lat. cognitionem) and "discernment" (Gr. διακρίσεως / diakriseōs / Lat. dijudicationem) must, however, be carefully examined. To do this, we will invoke an example provided by Saint Gregory of Nyssa, as he speaks about the precious metal, gold:

> The beauty of the substance seems good to those who love money: yet "the love of money is a root of all evil [1 Timothy 6:10]."[11]

Any metal or precious stone can be the object of the passion of someone possessed by the vice of greed. Thus, gold will not represent for the one possessed by this vice anything other than the object intended to increase their material wealth. Their entire reasoning only considers the means by which they can achieve their goal. Their knowledge is, in a word, deficient: they are never capable of understanding the profound, symbolic meanings of a precious metal like gold. What would, therefore, a gold-obsessed person say about the description of the heavenly Jerusalem from the Revelation of Saint John, chapter 21, verse 18, where we learn that "the city was pure gold, like clear glass"? Blinded by their own passion, they would neither be capable

[11] Ibid.

of nor desire to discern the divine reasons for this mention of gold, which, in the glorious period of Christian civilization, was used to decorate churches and icons, rather than to increase personal wealth. What blinds the miser is his knowledge tainted by his own passion: gold is for him nothing more than the support of a true illusion, the deception in which he is ensnared.

To clarify, as much as possible, this interpretation, I will outline a theory of knowledge inspired by a brief commentary from one of the most important doctors from the golden age of Christian thought, Saint Gregory of Nazianzus. A good friend of Saints Basil the Great and Gregory of Nyssa, he commented on the same issue discussed by Saint Gregory of Nyssa: the nature of the two trees in Paradise. The discussion begins with a description of man's state in Paradise, tested by God through the first commandment (law) entrusted to him:

> He gave him a Law, as a material for his Free Will to act upon. This Law was a Commandment as to what plants he might partake of, and which one he might not touch. This latter was the Tree of Knowledge; not, however, because it was evil from the beginning when planted; nor was it forbidden because God grudged it to us . . . Let not the enemies of God wag their tongues in that

> direction, or imitate the Serpent... But it would have been good if partaken of at the proper time, for *the tree was, according to my theory, Contemplation*, upon which it is only safe for those who have reached maturity of habit to enter; but which is not good for those who are still somewhat simple and greedy in their habit; just as solid food is not good for those who are yet tender, and have need of milk [Hebrews 5:12].[12]

The commentary proposed by Gregory of Nazianzus clarifies, through the recourse to the concept of "contemplation," the theory of knowledge developed by his friend, Gregory of Nyssa. He specifies how, depending both on the moment when the cognitive/contemplative act occurs and on its orientation, the consequences can be positive or negative. Thus, the act of knowing any creature could be performed by Adam and Eve in two radically different ways. The first, in accordance with the principle of original righteousness, *seeks the divine reasons* in the entire creation. This type of theocentric contemplation discovers God, the Creator,

[12] Gregory of Nazianzus, [*Oration 38*], trans. Charles Gordon Browne and James Edward Swallow, in *Nicene and Post-Nicene Fathers*, ed. Philip Schaff and Henry Wace, Second Series, vol. 7 (Buffalo, NY: Christian Literature Publishing, 1893). Emphasis added. Available online here: http://www.newadvent.org/fathers/310238.htm.

everywhere, even when scrutinizing creatures. Another form of contemplation is equally possible, however, usually simply called "knowledge," which, ignoring the Creator, gets caught in the crushing grip of the pleasure/pain dichotomy. Maximizing this type of knowledge and excluding theocentric contemplation is what the devil pursued through the temptation of Eve. The episode highlights an overemphasis on the external, stimulating qualities of the forbidden fruit—"good to eat, and fair to the eyes, and delightful to behold" (Genesis 3:6)—at the expense of its profound, divine origin.

Let's look at an illustrative example taken from Mark Twain's famous story, *The Prince and the Pauper*. Many readers probably remember the amusing moment when the beggar, swapped for the heir prince due to his resemblance, cracks nuts with the Great Seal of the Kingdom. Here, an invaluable artifact, the symbolic value of which far exceeded the value of the gold it was made of, could be destroyed due to *the deficient knowledge* of the one using it! The beggar lacked the maturity of understanding that would have allowed him to appreciate the symbolic value of the object in question. Similarly, the contemplation of any part of creation could be performed by Adam and Eve in two radically different ways. The first, in accordance with the principle of original righteousness, would have sought the divine meaning. This is the *theological contemplation* that discovers the Creator everywhere, even when scrutinizing creatures. However, this way of knowing requires uninterrupted asceticism and patient effort from the one who performs it. At the same time, the bodily dimension of humans makes possible natural contemplation, influenced by the dichotomy of pleasure and pain. This is exactly what the devil counted on when tempting Eve through the serpent. The temptation is entirely characterized by exaggeration, by an overemphasis on the sensory qualities of the forbidden fruit:

> And the woman saw that the tree was good to eat, and fair to the eyes, and delightful to behold. (Genesis 3:6)[13]

Strongly marked by emotions and feelings of an unprecedented magnitude, Eve contemplates the creatures in a "consumerist" manner that no longer takes into account their divine reasons and God's command. As one might say, instead of receiving the fruit at the right time from God's hand, she receives the fruit at the wrong time from the devil's hand. However, it all depended on how the

[13] *Biblia Sacra Juxtam Vulgatam Clementinam*, 7, The Latin text: "Vidit igitur mulier quod bonum esset lignum ad vescendum, et pulchrum oculis, aspectuque delectabile."

human intellect's capacity *to know* was used: just like Eve, for the passionate person who forgets the reasons for things and beings created by God, the intellect becomes a slave to his or her own passions. The thief, the greedy person, or the lustful person subordinates his mind and reason to the act of deficient, darkened knowledge, seeking only to satisfy his desires. For the first time, this suicidal way of knowing was practiced by Eve and Adam in Paradise. However, for the righteous person, a lover of the virtuous life, the mind is obediently and prayerfully subjected to the supernatural light of the divine intellect, which is the only guide in the act of truly knowing creation in all its beauties.

Consequently, the same act of contemplation becomes an occasion for spiritual growth—which would have led Adam and Eve to perfection and, ultimately, to the beatific vision. Thus, knowledge can lead to eternal life when it consistently seeks the uncreated, unifying light of divine wisdom, or conversely to eternal death when it is degraded to the level of predominantly sensory, passionate knowledge that is guided only by the obsessive, hedonistic, and lawless search for bodily pleasures.

Take the legend of King Midas of Phrygia. As the old Greek stories relate, driven by greed, King Midas sought and acquired the miraculous power to transform everything he touched into gold. Only starvation followed, as consequence. For the foolish king was to learn from experience that his thoughtless desire led to the transformation of everything—including the food and drink he touched—into gold. If we transpose this tale onto the theological world of the tree of the knowledge of good and evil, we could say that precisely that act of knowledge *not* guided by the light of divine wisdom was similar to Midas's touch: everything that was touched was transformed, as a punishment for disobedience to the divine command, into perishable matter, lacking receptivity to grace. This transitioned to a mode of being destined for a life suspended between the absence of Being and the deceptive evanescence of Nothingness. To better clarify all these aspects, Saint Gregory of Nyssa resumes his reflections within the much rarer horizon of metaphysical speculations in the *Great Catechetical Discourse*—a work rightly considered his most important.

In this treatise, the distinction we know from the Creed will be postulated first, where, after professing the existence of the one God, we add that He is the creator of "the visible (ὁρατῶν / horatōn) and the invisible (ἀοράτων / aoratōn)." Saint Gregory of Nyssa explains that this distinction refers to the two realms of reality accessible to our minds: what we know through the senses, or the material, sensible, physical world, and what we know only with the help of the intellect, that is, the spiritual, intelligible, metaphysical world. This distinction, well known to the great Greek philosophers Plato and Aristotle as well as to the Neoplatonists, was recognized and fully assimilated by the great thinkers of the Christian Tradition. Saint Gregory of Nyssa clearly explains that "the world of thought is bodiless, impalpable, and figureless; but the sensible is, by its very name, bounded by those perceptions which come through the organs of sense."[14]

Thus, the world is composed of a harmonious blend between the two planes of existence, the sensible and the intelligible, just as in man we find the same structure: the body represents the physical, material dimension of man, while the soul represents his spiritual, intelligible dimension. Although human nature is unique, this unity of its two dimensions transforms it into a true synthesis of all creation, a synthesis that encompasses both the lower realms (recapitulated in the body)

[14] Gregory of Nyssa, *Great Catechetical Discourse*, trans. William Moore and Henry Austin Wilson, in *Nicene and Post-Nicene Fathers*, ed. Philip Schaff and Henry Wace, Second Series, vol. 5 (Buffalo, NY: Christian Literature Publishing, 1893). Available online here: https://www.newadvent.org/fathers/29082.htm.

and the angelic, superior ones, existing in the soul endowed with intellect. The major problem our author will face, after postulating this hierarchical existence that reveals the two distinct levels of the created world—intelligible (spiritual) and sensible (material)—is the emergence of evil in the first of the angels created by God. How was this possible? Here begins a series of grand metaphysical explanations, the only ones capable, to a limited extent, of offering clarifications regarding the fall of the rebellious angels and, later on, the fall of the first humans. The text of Saint Gregory of Nyssa deserves to be quoted in its entirety:

> But the question, how one who had been created for no evil purpose by Him who framed the system of the Universe in goodness fell away, nevertheless, into this passion of envy, it is not a part of my present business minutely to discuss; though it would not be difficult, and it would not take long, to offer an account to those who are amenable to persuasion. For the distinctive difference between virtue and vice is not to be contemplated as that between two actually subsisting phenomena; but as there is a logical opposition between that which is [=Being] and that which is not [=Nothingness], and it is not possible to say that, as regards subsistency, that which is not is distinguished from that which is, but we say

> that nonentity is only logically opposed to entity, in the same way also the word vice is opposed to the word virtue, not as being any existence in itself, but only as becoming thinkable by the absence of the better. As we say that blindness is logically opposed to sight, not that blindness has of itself a natural existence, being only a deprivation of a preceding faculty, so also we say that vice is to be regarded as the deprivation of goodness, just as a shadow which supervenes at the passage of the solar ray.[15]

In these lines, we discern an entire metaphysical doctrine about the origin of evil, which also offers us, as we shall see, the elucidating framework regarding the nature of the trees in Eden and original sin. The idea of the shadow that immediately falls when the light passes away has a particularly special value. Just as, in the case of the rebellious angel, ignoring the Supreme Good leads to the emergence of evil, in the case of Adam and Eve, ignoring the contemplation of the sole Creator of all creatures in an act of knowledge that seeks to embrace the sensible world without seeking the profound, divine reasons of things, will lead to the loss of the supernatural light of grace and the plunge into the darkness of becoming and death.

[15] Ibid.

How could the angel consumed by envy provoke such an act of rebellion in the first humans? Saint Gregory of Nyssa explains:

> Yet could he not by any exercise of strength or dint of force accomplish his purpose, for the strength of God's blessing overmastered his own force. His plan, therefore, is to withdraw man from this enabling strength, that thus he may be easily captured by him and open to his treachery. As in a lamp when the flame has caught the wick and a person is unable to blow it out, he mixes water with the oil and by this devices will dull the flame, in the same way the enemy, by craftily mixing up badness in man's will, has produced a kind of extinguishment and dullness in the blessing, on the failure of which that which is opposed necessarily enters.[16]

Here we have retold, in terms of his metaphysics, the entire unfolding of the temptation and fall that occurred in Eden. The devil realized, therefore, that he could not extinguish the light of the sanctifying grace of original justice—symbolized by the flame of the lamp—directly, through his own powers. So, employing his cunning, he mixed into the oil of the lamp, which symbolizes the well-created nature of

[16] Ibid.

man, with water, which would lead to the extinguishing of the light. Centuries later, another great saint and doctor of the church, Francis de Sales, would refine Saint Gregory of Nyssa's image to explain how a person can come to lose the fire of divine love:

> The heavens themselves are astonished, their gates become desolate with fear, and the angels of peace are lost in amazement at this prodigious misery of man's heart, abandoning a good so worthy of love, to join itself to things so unworthy. But have you never seen that little marvel which everyone knows, though everyone does not know the reason of it? When a very full barrel is broached, the wine will not run unless it has air given from above.[17]

In both explanations, we encounter the same main idea: sanctifying grace—symbolized by Saint Gregory of Nyssa as the light of the lamp and by Saint Francis de Sales as the wine kept in a barrel—is removed by the introduction of a foreign element that instantly drives it out. To reinforce this explanation, the first of them will revisit it using another poignant image:

[17] Francis de Sales, *Library of Saint Francis de Sales*, vol. 2, Treatise on the love of God (London: Burns and Oates; New York: Benziger, 1910), 166.

> We supposed that some vessel has been composed of clay, and then, for some mischief or other, filled with melted lead, which lead hardens and remains in a non-liquid state; then that the owner of the vessel recovers it, and, as he possesses the potter's art, pounds to bits the ware which held the lead, and then remolds the vessel after its former pattern for his own special use, emptied now of the material which had been mixed with it: by a like process the maker of our vessel, now that wickedness has intermingled with our sentient part, I mean that connected with the body, will dissolve the material which has received the evil, and, remolding it again by the Resurrection without any admixture of the contrary matter, will recombine the elements into the vessel in its original beauty.[18]

Molten lead is the symbol of that foreign element, evil, which, once it penetrates human nature, will immediately cause the loss of sanctifying grace. And this loss has as an inevitable consequence—not only inevitable but also foretold by God Himself—the loss of eternal youth and everlasting life. All these comments echo the famous verses from the book of Wisdom of Solomon (chapter 2, verses 23–24):

[18] Gregory of Nyssa, *Great Catechetical Discourse.*

> God created man incorruptible, and to the image of his own likeness he made him. But by the envy of the devil, death came into the world.[19]

Immortal through the work of grace and the preternatural gifts associated with it, man was deceived by the devil-serpent to taste the forbidden fruit. This food introduced into human nature that foreign element, evil, symbolized by the molten lead hardened in a vessel, by the water that extinguishes the lamp's flame once mixed with the oil, and by the air that, once allowed into the barrel, forces out the wine. All these are the direct consequence of consuming the forbidden fruit—knowledge of good mixed with evil—through the willful violation of the divine commandment. Instead of strengthening himself in the contemplation of Divine Wisdom manifested in the diversity of creatures whose profound reasons Adam was supposed to know, prompted by Eve—who was herself deceived by the serpent—Adam replaces supernatural contemplation with an act of knowledge predominantly based on the senses and exclusively oriented by the terrible pleasure-pain

[19] *Biblia Sacra Juxtam Vulgatam Clementinam*, 718. The Latin text: "Quoniam Deus creavit hominem inexterminabilem, et ad imaginem similitudinis suae fecit illum. Invidia autem diaboli mors introivit in orbem terrarum: imitantur autem illum qui sunt ex parte illius."

dichotomy, which seems to have become the sole meaning of human existence.

Saint Athanasius the Great, with Saints Gregory of Nyssa and Gregory of Nazianzus, explains the same Old Testament episode by invoking the metaphysical terms of being (τὸ ὄν) and non-being (οὐκὄν). He leads us to a better understanding of the tree of the knowledge of good and evil with his definitions of being and non-being in his treatise, *Against the Heathen*:

> Good is, while evil is not; by what is [=Being], then, I mean what is good, inasmuch as it has its pattern in God Who is. But by what is not [=Nothingness] I mean what is evil, in so far as it consists in a false imagination in the thoughts of men.[20]

The consequence of these definitions is inevitable. The tree of the knowledge of "good and evil" can be interpreted as the tree of the knowledge of "being and nothingness." Yet, if God himself created the

[20] Athanasius the Great, *Against the Heathen*, trans. Archibald Robertson, in *Nicene and Post-Nicene Fathers*, ed. Philip Schaff and Henry Wace, Second Series, vol. 4 (Buffalo, NY: Christian Literature Publishing, 1892). Available online here: https://www.newadvent.org/fathers/2801.htm. Here is the original Greek text: ὄντα δέφημιτὰ καλά, καθότι ἐκ τοῦ ὄντος Θεοῦ τὰ παραδείγματα ἔχει· οὐκὄντα δὲ τὰ κακὰ λέγω, καθότι ἐπινοίαις ἀνθρώπων οὐκὄντα ἀναπέπλασται. Patrologia Graeca, Tomus XXV (n.p.: Jacques Paul Migne), column 9.

world out of nothing (*ex nihilo*), how can the original nothingness be identified with evil? In fact, we are dealing with two types of nothingness. The first is the "formless and void earth" (Genesis 1:2), from which God created everything that exists. He did this by covering the "nothingness" of creatures with the light of His uncreated grace. The second type of "nothingness," evil, represents the nothingness of creatures *revealed through the exclusion of sanctifying grace*. It is evil because it is the result of an attempted deicide: the creature attempts to design/create a world from which the Creator is excluded. The difference between the two forms of nothingness is radical. We know very well that when God contemplated creation, He saw that "everything was very good." There was no evil, no stain, no shadow in the freshly conceived things. The reason for that state—which, although perfectible, was (almost) ideal—was linked to the "covering" each creature had through the light of grace. Everything that existed was created by God to breathe the fragrant and luminous air of original righteousness. Rightfully, that state could be called "Paradise."

If I were to represent everything through a symbolic image, I would say that, initially, man created from nothing was, at the soul level, clothed in the garment of sanctifying grace, while at the bodily level he was like a well-polished crystal (or diamond) that allowed light to pass through him to bless the entire surrounding world. Man had no shadow and was not ashamed of his "nakedness." However, the Fall immediately caused the withdrawal of the light of grace and the transformation of the body into an opaque mass. From that moment, man casts a shadow on the earth through his body corrupted by mortality, a body that acts like the gravitational force keeping us attached to mundane, non-transparent matter. As I showed previously, Saint Gregory of Nyssa represented this terrible episode in human history using another symbolic image: that of the vessel which, initially, was full of the noble content of grace, but after the original sin, "poured out" the sanctifying light to be filled with the devil's molten lead, i.e., biological, mortal life devoid of the Supernatural Good of the paradisiacal world.

The key to understanding this mutation is provided by *a transformative knowledge*. Like in the story of King Midas, it is a knowledge that influences the quality of nature, which is the foundation of both humanity and all creation. A contemplative act, as already mentioned, can be directed towards discovering the Creator—through the divine reasons (the "logoi," as Saint Maximus the Confessor calls them) of all creatures—in all that exists, or, on the contrary, towards the contemplation of one's own body, one's own ego, and his unruly passions reflected in everything that is. Such a vision led Saint Athanasius the Great to focus his commentary on the Fall on the notion of contemplation:

> God has made man, and willed that he should abide in incorruption; but men, having despised and rejected the contemplation of God, and devised and contrived evil for themselves, received the condemnation of death with which they had been threatened; and from thenceforth no longer remained as they were made, but were being corrupted according to their devices; and death had the mastery over them as king [Romans 5:14]. For transgression of the commandment was turning them back to their natural state, so that just as they have had their being out of nothing, so also, as might be expected, they might look for corruption into nothing in the course of time. For if, out of a former normal state of non-existence, they were called into being by the Presence and loving-kindness of the Word, it followed naturally that when men were bereft of the knowledge of God and were turned back to what was not (for what is evil is not, but what is good is), they should, since they derive their being from God who is, be everlastingly bereft even of being; in

> other words, that they should be disintegrated and abide in death and corruption. For man is by nature mortal, inasmuch as he is made out of what is not; but by reason of his likeness to Him that is (and if he still preserved this likeness by keeping Him in his knowledge) he would stay his natural corruption, and remain incorrupt; as Wisdom [6:18] says: "The taking heed to His laws is the assurance of immortality"; but being incorrupt, he would live henceforth as God, to which I suppose the divine Scripture refers, when it says: "I have said you are gods, and you are all sons of the most Highest; but you die like men, and fall as one of the princes."[21]

After presenting the interpretations of Saints Gregory of Nyssa, Gregory of Nazianzus, and Athanasius the Great, I will summarize the guiding ideas of the entire hermeneutic context, which will allow us to answer the question raised by Horia-Roman Patapievici: "Where did paradise go?"[22]

[21] Athanasius the Great, *On the Incarnation of the Word*. Translated by Archibald Robertson, in *Nicene and Post-Nicene Fathers*, Second Series, Vol. 4. Edited by Philip Schaff and Henry Wace (Buffalo, NY: Christian Literature Publishing Co., 1892). Revised and edited for New Advent by Kevin Knight: https://www.newadvent.org/fathers/2802.htm.

[22] Horia-Roman Patapievici, *Două eseuri despre Paradis* [Two essays on paradise] (Bucharest: Humanitas, 2018). His reflections on what he calls the "principle of Paradise" are contained therein.

Using one of the most valuable metaphors appropriate to the current state of human nature, developed by Plato in the dialogue *Phaedo*[23] and by Saint Maximus the Confessor in *Quaestiones ad Thalassium* (*Questions Addressed to Thalassius,* question 64), man transitioned from a life lived in the luminous atmosphere of Paradise to the underwater life of a being submerged in the depths of the ocean. The essences of things and their divine reasons became inaccessible to knowledge "stuck" to the surface of things. These, like the human body, became opaque, as if covered with a crust that makes the "core" of their intelligibility hard to access. The "tunics of skin" (Genesis 3:21) have, in a certain sense, the function of a diving suit that makes life possible, temporarily, in a hostile, corrupt, and continually changing environment. How did this happen, in detail?

At the bodily level, nature transitioned from a state of clarity, transparency, and preternatural subtlety generated by the workings of the graces with which it was adorned, to a mortiferous state, in which humors and cells are in a state of entropy. It is a slow dissolution, as we see in the processes of growth, aging, and, finally, death. Neither the earthly science of metaphysical ignorants nor the

[23] 109b ff.

billions invested by companies seeking the secret of youth and immortality will ever succeed in stopping this flow of degeneration. The soul, on the other hand, being immortal, entered a state in which high contemplation became practically inaccessible. The simple and direct knowledge of the intelligible world and of God ceased. As Saint Hildegard of Bingen says, man has gone blind. For he can no longer see the unseen world. Instead, the deep energies of the intellect underwent a process of perversion: strictly oriented towards the material world, they were subordinated either to sensory knowledge that generates, as Aristotle and Saint Thomas say, phantasms, or to rational knowledge which, although eminent, is deficient and powerless in the absence of mystical intuitions and high contemplation. The soul has been "clothed" in the terrible garment of concupiscence, marked by irrational desires that pull it in all directions, exhausting it. Imagination, or the "internal sense" that collects the phantasms generated by the empiric knowledge, represents the most serious obstacle to contemplation. Even when imagination is well-formed, it is only a shadow of the contemplation of the intelligible realities to which we no longer have direct access.

But it all begins, let us remember, with poorly oriented knowledge, which instead of focusing on the noble, subtle, and profound part of the things in the world created by God, seeks only to satisfy desires through pleasures, inventing all sorts of tricks to avoid suffering, inevitable otherwise in such a ontologically degraded state of human being. As Saint Athanasius says, instead of heading towards an ontological plenitude, growing and receiving "grace upon grace," man headed towards the nothingness from which he was created, sliding down the slope of non-being.

Created in a state of perfectible goodness, he could relate to the surrounding world through an act of knowledge whose consequences depended on *the focal point* targeted by the sharp minds of our parents. If this reference point was and remained God, as in a perpetual prayer—or act of adoration—Adam and Eve would have kept our access to the sphere of uncreated Wisdom, the true Tree of Life that nourished their innocent souls with grace. Immortality was just one of the preternatural effects of the graces that were flooding this happy and beneficial mode of being. However, if their minds allowed themselves to be tempted by the material-empirical dimension of the world and their own corporeality, opting exclusively for sensory knowledge, seeking pleasure and avoiding pain, they consumed, as Saint Maximus the Confessor says (*Quaestiones ad Thalassium,* questio 43), the forbidden fruit of good and evil, of being and non-being.

As we know from the Holy Scripture, things happened in this second way. Instantly, the grace of the Great King was withdrawn, outraged by the offense of an idolatrous act of adoration whose object was creatures, not Him, the only Creator. The withdrawal of the veil of supernatural light that clothed the world led to what we see now: a deeply corrupted world and humanity, gnawed from within by the nothingness manifested in the terrifying form of the "shadow of death." Thus began the drama of fallen human history, both frivolous and tragic, in which Good and Evil—Being and Nothingness—confront each other until the righteous Creator decides that the time for the great and fearful judgment has come.

CHAPTER 7

Returning to Paradise

DANTE AND THE DOUBLE METAMORPHOSIS

As I have shown in previous chapters, saints such as Augustine, Basil the Great, Isidore of Seville, and Thomas Aquinas emphasize the real existence of Paradise, insisting on the historical-literal character of the biblical episode describing the original sin committed by Adam and Eve. However, today we are certain that Admiral Christopher Columbus never passed near the garden of eternal life in his travels. The terrestrial existence of an inaccessible place—due to its location on a mountaintop or through a supposed wall of fire that would prevent access to the interior—is illusory. Consequently, we are compelled to confront the key question: did Paradise, at one time, truly exist? The answer, supported not only by sacred texts from various traditions but also by the mystical experiences of those who have seen it during their earthly lives, is categorically positive. So how can its absence from our physical world be explained? Where was it located?

In order to give a clear answer, I have to emphasize the unimaginable power of the divine grace and all the negative consequence of its disappearance from our world: the metaphor of a world *without* the sun is just a pale illustration of the negative consequences of the fall of Adam and Eve. Even though it is not satisfactory enough, the image of a world without light reminds us that the whole living world will die without it. Similarly, Paradise has become inaccessible and our world, devoid of the everlasting light of sanctifying grace, plunged into the dark ocean of death and nothingness. The consequences of this *mutation* are depicted by Saint Luke when he writes about "those who sit in darkness and in the shadow of death" (Luke 1:79).

As Saints Gregory of Nyssa and Athanasius the Great show us, both the world and the man have suffered a major ontological transformation that, without changing the nature proper to the creation and creatures, lead to the modification of the *qualities* or *the glory* of this nature: from spiritual, celestial, incorruptible and immortal, both the man and the creation have become material, earthly, corruptible and mortal. In his perennial teachings Saint Paul emphasizes that "there are bodies celestial, and bodies terrestrial: but, one is the glory of the celestial, and another of the terrestrial" (1 Corinthians 15: 41–44). After the original sin, the heavenly glory that covered all the creatures has been changed into a passing and earthly glory, specific to all those creatures destined to die.

The "mutation" of the physical world and of all the creatures—as a result of that terrible divine punishment: "cursed is the earth in thy work" (Genesis 3:17)—is depicted in the verses 16, 17 and 18 of the 3rd chapter of the Book of Genesis. Saint Paul summarizes this cosmic event in his letter to the Romans (8:20), where he shows that "the creature was made subject to vanity, not willingly, but by reason of him (i.e., the man) that made it subject." From these biblical texts we can understand, together with Saint Augustine and Theodoret of Cyrus, that after the fall of Adam and Eve not just the human beings, but the whole creation and all the creatures were enslaved to death, too. In this way, thc world has changed its manner of being from the full-of-grace Paradise to the desert existence of the mortals. Being in this fallen state any of us can say, together with King David, that "my life hath drawn nigh to hell" (Psalm 87:4). Nothing from all the things that we can perceive through our senses can escape the gradual dissolution. If we meditate carefully we realize that even the most solid piece of granite is getting older and, one day, it will become dust. The Sahara dunes are the living testimony of this destructive process. Much more acute, however, our own bodies are also the living evidence of the ephemerality of both the fallen world and man. The older we get, the more we become aware of the inevitable decomposition process, which already affects us through weaknesses, diseases, or infirmities of all kinds. All these vicissitudes of our existence are the result of the absence of divine grace which enlightened Paradise.

The Saxon master Hugo of Saint Victor (1096–1141) says that if it had not fallen the whole would have been *entirely* Paradise. Viewed from this perspective, therefore, the Garden of Eden does not represent a part of this world—a part which has become *physically* inaccessible, by its location on the top of a mountain or by a supposed wall of fire that would impede access inside—but it symbolizes *the world as a whole*. Enlightened by divine grace, the entire world would become a Paradise full of that unspeakable joy lived before the Fall. After the original sin, the entire world has become a sort of theatre of shadows similar to that depicted in Plato's myth of the cavern. Paradise has become inaccessible though a "mutation" of the physical world's qualities. This process is the consequence of the corruption of human nature, initiated at the moment of the original sin.

Probably the most fitting metaphor to describe this mutation is that of a photographic negative. As all photography enthusiasts well know, the film obtained initially after the first chemical processes contains only an inverted black-and-white representation: what is bright in reality appears dark, and what is dark appears bright. To obtain a photograph, additional chemical processes are needed for the "revelation" of the true image. The key element in the entire process is silver. Similarly, through original sin, the key element—divine grace—was immediately lost. This grace had shown the world as it was conceived and created *ab initio* by God. In the absence of this element, the world became exactly what the negative of a photograph is: a place of shadows, where good and evil, being and nothingness, intermingle, creating a play of deceptive shadows.

Man has lost access to the Tree of Life—which is nothing else but the grace of divine wisdom (Proverbs 3:18) accessible through contemplation. Based on what Saint Gregory of Nazianzus says, this contemplation made possible the immortality of the inhabitants of Eden (Wisdom 6:13–20). The access to Paradise became impossible due to a serious alteration of the act of knowledge which, instead of seeking in all creatures their divine reasons, became a kind of passionate embrace of earthly things for purely "consumeristic" purposes. Such an attitude of the intellect is the direct consequence of pride manifested through the Mephistophelian claim to be like God (Genesis 3:5).

As a result of this rebellious act—*peccato originali*—which can be better summarized by using the Greek notion of *hybris* (ὕβρις), the human intellect was instantly "blinded" by losing the light of divine grace that gave Adam and Eve the preternatural (= beyond ordinary nature) qualities inherent to a life without death: impassibility (no diseases, injuries, infirmities), integrity of passions (a complete submission of the passions to the reason), agility (a body that can move—so to say—at the speed of thought), subtlety (a body which is "spiritual" and "celestial" as Saint Paul teaches in 1 Corinthians 15:40–49) and brightness (a state full of light of grace).[1]

[1] A detailed exposition of the preternatural and supernatural privileges of man in the pre-lapsarian state or in the state of eternal happiness after the resurrection of the bodies can be found in Ludwig Ott's *Fundamentals of Catholic Dogma* (TAN Books, 1960), 101–6.

Man was exiled from Paradise (Genesis 3:224) because he perverted—by a decision of his own free will—his capacity for contemplation which makes Eden visible to those whose intellects are illuminated by eternal Wisdom. Here, then, is how Paradise became inaccessible to mortals: *subjectively*, by losing the light of the divine wisdom, which alone makes us able to see it; *objectively*, by the transformation of the created world which, without grace, becomes opaque, evanescent, pure materialistic. Consequently, the difference between our current *fallen* nature and the nature of Adam and Eve *before* their transgression is really enormous.

Before their transgression they were immersed in the supernatural light of divine grace which gave them immortality. The world, too, was free of those vicissitudes inherent in degradation, corruption, death. The inner being of man was enlightened by all those qualities specific to the Tree of Life (divine wisdom) which were interiorized by an act of contemplation that was as natural to the first people as it is for us to gaze at a wonderful sunset. Even though they had not yet come to the so called "beatific vision" of God, Adam and Eve could know Him the way we can see a reflection of our faces in a crystal pool. But that heavenly knowledge of Adam and Eve still had a dose of imperfection: it could be trapped within the material dimension of the world—if it were not maintained at the level of contemplating the deep, divine reasons of all created beings.

The serpent tested the firmness of Adam's intellectual-contemplative capacity to remain perpetually attached, with humility, to the single and absolute point of reference of any act of knowledge: God. The "forbidden fruit"—the world and all the creatures known *without* God, as Saint Maximus the Confessor teaches us—was chosen because of that incredible lie by which the devil made Eve believe that she may be like God. The mere consent to such a suggestion led to the immediate withdrawal, from the heart of man and from the depths of the whole creation, of the divine grace. Both man and world plunged into darkness.

The exclusion from Paradise occurred in the blink of an eye. Adam and Eve were instantly assaulted by the shameful passions of the flesh in their rebellion against reason. In a word, their souls died. This new and tragic status became manifest through the complete loss of access to the contemplation of divine wisdom that made them immortal. The Tree of Life had become completely inaccessible to them. Their souls were reduced to the stage of a vegetative, animal life, now enslaved to their earthly, mortal bodies. Faced with such a miserable situation, the sages of history have faced and are faced with one essential and unavoidable question: how can immortality and life in Paradise be restored?

Similar to many other Catholic thinkers, the famous Florentine poet, Dante Alighieri (1265–1321), reflected throughout his entire life on the possibility of returning to Paradise. One of the most brilliant contemporary Romanian thinkers, Horia-Roman Patapievici describes with remarkable clarity Dante's ideas as expressed by his journey to Paradise in the *Divine Comedy*:

> First, Dante "re-formed" himself, then "transubstantiated" his nature.... To be able to enter the first heaven of the heavenly paradise, which is visible, but is spiritual, Dante had to "trans-humanize" himself: *transumanare* (in Italian) is a notion invented by Dante in order to express, by analogy with a transformation of man into a god narrated by Ovid in *Metamorphoses*, how he also changed, at the entrance to the heavenly paradise, the "formal" data of his human nature. The second transformation takes place at the physical entrance to the Empyrean Heaven. In order to physically enter the Empyrean Heaven, in the great invisible sky of the visible heavenly paradise, Dante also had to change the "matter" of his human condition: and this is done through an operation that is

> a sort of an analogous notion to the Christian trans-substantiation of the Eucharist.[2]

Actually, these two stages of Dante's journey through Paradise indicate a double meta-morphosis of those who seek to reach the heavenly Jerusalem. This double metamorphosis — or, in Dante's words, "trans-humanization" — of the fallen human nature will finally lead to the so-called "beatific vision" of the Living God adored by Dante and all Christians. Such a high status of the soul will be accessible just after the universal judgment and resurrection of the bodies. But the first metamorphosis, accessible here and now to all Christians, can restore in us partially those qualities of Adam and Eve before the Fall. This fact is proven by the amazingly uncorrupted bodies of saints like Vincent de Paul, Bernadette Soubirous, Catherine Labouré, Louise de Marillac and Rafaela Porras Ayllón.[3]

The return to the Lost Paradise begins from this life, through our re-planting, performed by

[2] Horia-Roman Patapievici, *Două eseuri despre Paradis* [Two essays on paradise] (Bucharest: Humanitas, 2018), 31 (my translation). Both on page 83 and in a note on page 105, Patapievici shows that the Italian term *trans-umanare* ("trans-humanization"), coined by Dante, appears in the *Divine Comedy*, Paradise, I, 70–72.

[3] A work that presents most of the cases of incorruptibility recorded in the annals of the church is Joan Carroll Cruz's *The Incorruptibles* (TAN Books, 1977).

holy baptism, in the heavenly soil of eternal Jerusalem. Saints Cyprian of Carthage and Hippolytus of Rome postulate that all baptized Christians are through divine grace "plants rooted in the spiritual heaven." Based on this, the double "metamorphosis" or "trans-humanization" find their start in this life with the help of those means well known to Dante: the sacraments of the church (especially baptism, confession and Holy Eucharist). The context of a prayerful and contemplative life is another spiritual requirement that we are not allowed to forget. As for Divine Wisdom, the Tree of Life, let us remember: it is the highest gift of the Holy Spirit given to us through the sacrament of confirmation.

ROBERT LAZU KMITA (b. 1971) is a novelist, essayist, and columnist with a PhD in Philosophy. His first novel, *The Island without Seasons*, was published in 2023. He is also the author and coordinator of numerous books, including an *Encyclopedia of J.R.R. Tolkien's World* in Romanian. His articles have appeared in *VoegelinView*, *The Imaginative Conservative*, *The Remnant*, *Saint Austin Review*, *Polonia Christiana*, *Gregorius Magnus*, *Second Spring*, *Radici Cristiane*, and *Philosophy Today*, among other publications. Robert publishes regularly at his Substack, Kmita's Library.

www.ingramcontent.com/pod-product-compliance
Lightning Source LLC
LaVergne TN
LVHW090615110826
845146LV00001B/394

* 9 7 9 8 8 9 2 8 0 1 7 1 3 *